things
might go
terribly,
horribly
wrong

a guide to life liberated from anxiety

KELLY G. WILSON, PhD
TROY DUFRENE

New Harbinger Publications, Inc.

Publisher's Note

NEW HARBINGER PUBLICATIONS is a registered trademark of New Harbinger Publications, Inc.

Distributed in Canada by Raincoast Books

Copyright © 2010 by Kelly G. Wilson & Troy DuFrene
New Harbinger Publications, Inc.
5674 Shattuck Avenue
Oakland, CA 94609
www.newharbinger.com

Acquired by Catharine Sutker; Cover design by Amy Shoup; Edited by Nelda Street

"What We Knew," by Carolyn Elkins, from Daedalus Rising, Emrys Press, 2002, reprinted by permission of the author.

My Way
English Words by Paul Anka; Original French Words by Gilles Thibault
Music by Jacques Revaux and Claude François
Copyright © 1967 Societe Des Nouvelles and Editions Eddie Barclay
Copyright © 1969 Chrysalis Standards, Inc.
Copyright Renewed
All Rights for the USA Administered by Chrysalis Standards, Inc., Editions Jeune Musique, Warner Chappell Music France, Jingoro Co. and Architectural Music Co.
All Rights Reserved   Used by Permission
Reprinted by permission of Hal Leonard Corporation

Library of Congress Cataloging-in-Publication Data

Wilson, Kelly G.
  Things might go terribly, horribly wrong : a guide to life liberated from anxiety / Kelly G. Wilson and Troy DuFrene.
    p. cm.
  Includes bibliographical references.
  ISBN 978-1-57224-711-6
  1. Anxiety. 2. Anxiety--Treatment. 3. Acceptance and commitment therapy. I. DuFrene, Troy, 1972- II. Title.
  BF575.A6.W55 2010
  152.4'6--dc22   2010000225

For my wife Dianna, after thirty years,
on this very day, I choose you.

—K. G. W.

To chance, because sometimes things
go wonderfully, fabulously right.

—T. D.

Contents

Things We Want to Say

Don't let the covers fool you. Books, like lives, are wiggling, evolving, living things. They're not bound by pages or authors or schools of thought. They're not born when they're printed; in fact, they only start to live once they're read. So first of all, we thank you, reader. You dignify this work we do, and we're sincerely grateful for your time and attention.

Acceptance and commitment therapy (ACT) is fundamentally and significantly a community effort. Our thanks go out to everyone who contributes to this work, its development, and its dissemination. In particular, thanks to the folks in Kelly's lab at Ole Miss and to all of our teachers, wherever they may now be.

We're grateful to the folks at New Harbinger for shepherding the book through its long and tortuous gestation, especially to Catharine Sutker, Jess Beebe, and Nelda Street. And we particularly thank Heather Mitchener, who has a future in talking would-be jumpers down from ledges if this whole editorial thing doesn't work out for her.

Finally, and most importantly, we offer our thanks and love to our families—to Dianna, Chelsea, Emma, Sarah, and the rest—whose indulgence and support make it possible for us to get up to these shenanigans, scribbling books when, by rights, we should be paying more attention to them.

1

Things
Might Go
Terribly,
Horribly
Wrong

But, Mousie, thou art no thy lane,

In proving foresight may be vain;

The best-laid schemes o' mice an' men

Gang aft agley,

An'lea'e us nought but grief an' pain,

For promis'd joy!*

—Robert Burns, "To a Mouse"

One Tuesday morning in 2001, a wine salesman was getting ready for work in his Berkeley, California, apartment. After showering and shaving, he put on an ill-fitting pin-striped suit, scuffed black loafers, and a blue tie that, he noted with alarm, had picked up a grease stain at lunch the day before. Because he worked in the city of San Francisco and the traffic from Berkeley into the city could sometimes be bad, he was in the habit of getting up early to avoid the worst of it. His girlfriend, with her more congenial commute, could afford an extra hour of sleep and was still in bed.

The wine salesman, in his own estimation, just wasn't well-suited to his job. He wasn't the kind of person who could show up on a sales call, make a pitch, and then either take an order or leave empty handed without a care. For him, each rejection felt personal. Every "no" stung a little more than the last. He was ill-equipped to deal with the inevitable humiliation that bruised him each time the answer to "How many can I get you?" was "None today, thanks."

As he brushed his teeth, he rolled over in his head the names and faces of the San Francisco liquor-store owners who might reject him

*But Mouse, you are not alone, / In proving foresight may be vain: / The best-laid schemes of men and mice / Often go askew, / and leave us nothing but grief and pain, / For promised joy!

later in the day. As he did, he had trouble focusing on any one of them. It was as if they all started to share one face.

If they didn't buy, he would fall behind on his quotas, and that would mean more than just lost commission. He wasn't certain where he stood with his boss and his boss's boss. He had only been on the job for half a year. So far he had consistently hit all of his numbers, but each month felt like a greater struggle. From time to time, he got encouraging voice mails from the area manager, and he had even been commended for performance at the last sales meeting. But it was just a matter of time. If his bosses really knew how hard he had to push to make his quotas or how close he invariably came to failure in the last days of each month, they would turn him out onto the streets without a second thought.

And for the last couple of weeks, his superiors had been condemningly silent. The main office had gone quiet. What could that mean? It would be one thing if they were angry with him, if they badgered him about his numbers—but this silent treatment was just too much.

On Monday, the day before, the prospect of being rejected one more time had been more than he could handle. He had gone to his first appointment, parked the car six blocks away, and walked to the liquor store's side door. He even put his hand on the knob but couldn't turn it. He circled the block a couple of times, sweating, his heart pounding in his chest. But when he went back to the door, once again he found he couldn't open it and walk inside.

So he left. He drove up to Pacific Heights and sat for six straight hours in his parked car, staring out at Alcatraz, feeling like he was in his own, personal prison. Every two or three minutes, he dialed the number to his voice mail, punched in his password, and waited to hear—what? The condemning voice of his customer, demanding to know why he hadn't shown up? The strained yet contained voice of the area manager, calling him into the office for a little chat? Instead, he heard nothing. The computerized female voice on the other end of the line told him the one thing he dreaded most of all: "You have no new voice mail messages."

Between calls to his voice mail, his phone never rang and his pager never went off. He couldn't shake the feeling that something was going on out there and that he didn't have a clue what it was. And that's when he noticed that every few heartbeats, there was a little flutter in his chest, a missed beat.

How long could this go on? He knew in his head that he could do this job—or, at least, he could do the job if he could get rid of this constant feeling that—what? That he would be fired? Would be made to look like a fool? Wouldn't be able to pay his rent? He really didn't even know which bothered him more.

The salesman had snapped out of his rumination when he felt a sharp twinge and then tasted blood in his mouth. It had taken him a moment to realize that, while he had been obsessing about the day before, he had been biting his nails and had finally chewed his thumbnail down to the quick. He checked his watch to see that it was already a quarter to eight. *Damn it!* There would already be a huge backup at the toll plaza on the bridge.

Now, he tore around the house, gathering up his things. He picked up his briefcase, car keys, and a half-eaten piece of toast and turned toward the front door. Before he could put his hand on the doorknob, his girlfriend rushed from the bedroom and called out to him.

"Turn on the news," she stammered. "There's been a massive terrorist attack in New York."

> The real troubles in your life are apt to be things that never crossed your worried mind; the kind that blindside you at 4:00 p.m. on some idle Tuesday.
>
> —Mary Schmich, "Advice, Like Youth, Probably Just Wasted on the Young"

Find the Way Out by Finding the Way In

Sometimes things go terribly, horribly wrong. Sometimes this happens in ways we aren't prepared for. And sometimes it happens in ways we could never have taken seriously or even imagined.

We don't think you need a history lesson about the capacity the world has for falling short of our expectations, but we could easily give you one. In the poem that opens this chapter, Robert Burns puts a fine point on the matter: despite all the planning and hedging we do against the possibility of misfortune, where we expect joy, we often find only fear and pain.

And what's the consequence of this? Do we accept with calm and equanimity the possibility that things might go terribly, horribly wrong and set about living our lives? For many of us, the answer is no. We worry. We panic. We fear. Like fortune-tellers, we peer into the future and pore over the past, looking for something, anything, that might be an antidote to the unknown. Sometimes this tendency to worry and fear gets untethered from any particular outcome that threatens us. We begin to worry about worry and fear fear itself. We panic and then panic that we might, once again, experience panic.

In other words, we get anxious, and for some of us, anxiety becomes quite literally our purpose. We surrender everything to these feelings; they take over our lives entirely. In a very real sense, we don't have anxiety. It has us.

This book is about anxiety and the role it plays in your life. More importantly, it's about finding a way for you to break free from the constraints that anxiety has placed on you. This book proposes to help you find a way out of your struggle with anxiety.

But this doesn't mean we're going to help you get rid of anxiety. Instead of trying to get away from these feelings, we're going to ask you to climb inside them, sit calmly in that place, and look around. We're going to ask you to get a sense of what's going on in your body and mind in the very moment when you're feeling anxious. We're going to ask you to have those feelings and experiences—even welcome them—and then go on living your life in a way that matters to you.

And we realize that, especially if your life has been significantly impeded by worry, fear, and panic, this probably sounds like the worst idea ever. Anxiety has been a burden that you've carried for a long time, and you probably want more than anything to set it down. We understand that. But in the chapters that follow, we're going to suggest that attempts to push these feelings away will only bring them closer and bind them more tightly to you. Counterintuitive though it may seem, we're going to propose that the best way for you to break free from anxiety is to acknowledge it, embrace it, even seek it out. Though this might sound scary now, we promise that any hard stuff that follows will come with plenty of warning and more than a little bit of humor to help take the edge off. If you're willing to come along with us, we think we can start you off on a journey that will lead you to a new and wonderful place—even if it's a place where anxiety can be too.

In the chapters that follow, we're going to discuss the phenomenon of anxiety in a broad and, we hope, sometimes surprising way. We'll begin by taking a look at the labels we currently put on certain kinds of anxious behavior—terms you're likely familiar with, like panic attacks and generalized anxiety disorder. And then we'll explore how these labels can be misleading and how thinking about anxiety in terms of the function it performs in your life can be more useful in the service of liberating you from its effects. We'll also take a look at how certain facts about the way we think and use language incline all of us to experience anxiety to some extent.

Once we get that out of the way, our goal will be to help you find a way to live a rich and meaningful life in the presence of whatever your mind throws your way, including anxiety. To do this, we're going to introduce you to the basic ideas that make up acceptance and commitment therapy (ACT), a model of psychotherapy that's both growing in popularity and accruing sound support in basic and applied research.

Viewed through the lens of ACT, problems in life, such as anxiety, look a little different than you might be used to. Instead of seeing a problem like anxiety as something you "have," like a virus or a broken bone, ACT describes these problems in terms of your ability to function in six *process areas*. These process areas are kind of like the building blocks of our problems (and our successes) in living. If we examine a problem like anxiety in light of these, we can point to certain process breakdowns that might be contributing to the problem, getting between us and whatever it is that we want in life. With these in mind, we can make small adjustments to the way we do things or relate to our experiences. Taken as a whole, these changes can help us wring more richness and meaning out of our lives—without having to first control, manage, or get rid of any particular thoughts, feelings, or experiences.

One of the interesting things about this unusual way of looking at problems with living is that it tends to break down the distinctions we make between different problems. By describing it in terms of breakdowns in a few basic life processes, we find that anxiety actually has a lot in common with depression, anger, and feelings of purposelessness, isolation, or alienation, and so forth. We start to see that there are actually some common threads that run through the whole cloth of human suffering, of human experience on the whole. As you consider your experience of anxiety from an ACT point of view, you may find that it reveals things about other aspects of your life with which you may have struggled.

We'll walk you through the six process areas in ACT in chapters 3 through 8. In the order we'll discuss them, they are:

- *Contact with the present moment*—the ability to bring flexible, focused attention to what's happening in your life right here, right now

- *Defusion*—the ability to hold thoughts and stories about what's possible lightly, without taking them literally or assuming they are invariably true

- *Acceptance*—the ability to acknowledge and affirm all aspects of your life just as they are

- *Values*—the ability to choose and articulate those aspects of your life that matter to you

- *Committed action*—the ability to choose to act in ways that further your values and to gently turn back toward those values when you find yourself going in a different direction

- *Self-as-context*—the ability to see yourself as the dynamic and evolving setting in which your life unfolds instead of as a fixed set of ideas about who you are and what you might become

We should tell you at the outset that there's no magic to the order we've chosen for this discussion. You can think of each of these process areas as the facets of a gem: if you peer in through one, you'll see the other five reflected within it. None of the process areas is more important than the others. Each functions in your life constantly and continuously, and each plays a key role in your experience of anxiety and of the other aspects of your life.

We also want to reassure you that, despite its sometimes strange vocabulary, ACT, at its core, isn't especially complicated or esoteric. It articulates in new ways some concepts that have been associated with wisdom and happiness for a long, long time—and it ties them to some principles that come out of the scientific study of behavior. We're not going to spend much time in this book discussing the scientific foundation of this material. We'll recommend further resources for that kind of information in the back of the book, "Sources for Further Study," if you're interested.

For now, what we want you to know about ACT is that it proposes, in very clear and concrete ways, a means to living a richer, more fulfilling, more significant life. Expressed a little differently, the ACT process model will help you find ways to:

- Remain flexibly and purposefully connected to the present moment rather than be pulled into the unchangeable past or the unknowable future.

- Keep your thoughts about the world in perspective as just thoughts, your stories about yourself and the world in perspective as just stories.

- Accept with equanimity and relative good humor *all* aspects of your life, whether pleasant or painful, in or out of your control.

- Be free to choose and to articulate what you want your life to be about.

- Commit to doing things, both great and small, that will shape your life around your hopes, dreams, and values— and, perhaps more importantly, turn back to these same principles when you wander from them.

- Recognize your life as a place of great and unfolding possibilities rather than a set of confining, rigidly defined stories about who you are and what you might become.

Keeping an Eye on the Prize

Your skills in these six areas collectively contribute to *psychological flexibility*, a state in which you enjoy a broad range of behavioral possibilities and you're free to make choices and act in ways consistent with what you want your life to be about.

If you think about it the way you think about physical flexibility, you'll have the basic idea: If you do things like stretching, you can increase the ranges of motion your body is capable of, enabling you to do more things than you could when you were less flexible. Work at it and you can touch your toes, limbo lower, and even do the splits. Also, when things go physically wrong, you'll be more likely to be able to compensate, accommodate, and bounce back. By increasing your ability to function in the six process areas, you become more psychologically limber. With your greater flexibility, you'll be able to do more things than you could do before: negotiate crowds, participate in social functions, take risks, and so forth.

The concept of psychological flexibility might seem obvious to you. If it seems strange, don't worry. It'll become clearer as you read. The reason we're taking the time to talk about it now, though, is that psychological flexibility is the explicit goal of ACT. The goal isn't symptom reduction. It's not the overcoming of anxiety. The goal isn't to make you feel happier or better about yourself. Plain and simple, the purpose of this work is to give you more room in which to live a life that matters to you. The goal is to set you free— not free of anxiety in the sense that hard thoughts and feelings cease to exist, rather, free in the sense that they no longer set limits on your life.

All of us are born, some time passes, and then we die. The first and last events are largely beyond our control. The bit in the middle— that's where we get to have a say. It's your life, your one and only life. How will you live it? How *can* you live it? The poets propose a couple of options.

I cannot rest from travel: I will drink
Life to the lees: all times I have enjoyed
Greatly, have suffered greatly, both with those
That loved me, and alone...

—Alfred Lord Tennyson, "Ulysses"

For I have known them all already, known them all—
Have known the evenings, mornings, afternoons,
I have measured out my life with coffee spoons;
I know the voices dying with a dying fall
Beneath the music from a farther room.
So how should I presume?

—T. S. Eliot, "The Lovesong of J. Alfred Prufrock."

So, which do you pick? A life drunk to the lees, filled with great joy and great pain, or one measured in coffee spoons, bound up in nervous speculation, lived against the backdrop of other people's conversations? It's probably not hard to guess your answer to that question. A better one might be, which one *can* you pick?

Imagine three scenarios, one or more of which might be familiar to you:

- You'd like to go to the party, but you're afraid people will reject or dislike you.

- You'd like to start a family, but you can't shake the feeling that you won't be a good parent.

- You'd like to excel in your profession, but you're always struggling to meet deadlines, and worry that failure and disgrace await you in every meeting.

What attracts your attention in these three situations? Is it the fear, the unshakable feeling, and the struggle and worry? Or is it the conviviality of friends, the profound love of a parent for a child, and the satisfaction and rewards of a successful career? Would you rather work hard to get rid of the former or to embrace the latter? Or, a better question might be, which *have* you worked harder for in the past?

If you're like most people with a history of anxiety problems, your answer to the last question is unambiguous: you've worked very, very hard to get rid of feelings of worry, fear, uncertainty, and shame. And maybe you've done this work because it seemed as if you needed to eliminate these obstacles before you could go after those things you wanted in your life. But what if you didn't have to do that?

Imagine the previous scenarios, but with a slightly different focus:

- You go to a party *while* fearing that people might reject or dislike you, and you find that somehow you're big enough to carry fear with ease.

- You start a family *while* feeling that you might not be a good parent, and find that sweet moments with your children aren't diminished in the slightest by feelings of inadequacy.

- You excel in your profession, *all the while* struggling to meet deadlines and feeling as if failure and disgrace await you at every meeting, but when you begin to discuss your struggles and feelings, you find out that both the most and least successful people you know feel much the same.

Pretty big difference, isn't it? The second set of scenarios is certainly not all wine and roses. It hurts. It's scary. At the end of the day, you've suffered greatly—but you've also enjoyed the company of your friends, the thrill of watching your children grow up, and the accolades (and paychecks) that come with productive work.

The difference between the first and second set of scenarios lies in your ability to bend, stretch, and extend yourself in the directions you want to go, even when those directions seem fraught with peril. In other words, the difference between the two is the degree of psychological flexibility you exhibit as you engage in the act of living your life. Increasing that flexibility in the service of what you value is the sole goal of this book.

It won't happen easily or overnight. A lifetime of missing parties, fretting about the future, and sitting silently in meetings isn't often undone by reading anything or even by knowing anything. Knowing, though, can precede doing. If any of what we've written here gives you a little space to move, it can help you start to wiggle. Wiggling can lead to stretching, stretching to stepping, stepping to striding—and when you can stride off in the direction you choose, you're free.

ACT can't shield you from the things that might go wrong in your life. It can't protect you from disappointment, rejection, and loss. But ACT can help you open up to the richness of experience and connect with a sense of purpose and direction that might, to this point, have been obscured by your struggle with anxiety. It can show you how to find the space you need to live your life in a way that matters to you, even while you remain, as ever, at large in the world with its inestimable potential for both pain and joy.

Who We Are

To be honest, it's a long story. Kelly followed a circuitous route through life to become a behavior analyst, a professor in the University of Mississippi Department of Psychology, a therapist, and a major contributor to the development of ACT and its popularity as a clinical approach throughout the world. In addition to writing and teaching, he maintains a busy schedule of presentations, trainings, and workshops in the United States and around the world. He has a notable fondness for coffee, hats, guitars, and ocean swimming, especially with his wife and daughters.

Troy is a writer and self-confirmed generalist. He cowrote the book *Coping with OCD* in 2007 with psychologist and OCD expert Bruce Hyman. He currently splits his time between the San Francisco Bay Area and Austin, Texas, with his wife and two spoiled pugs.

Through peculiar circumstance and unusually good fortune, Troy happened to attend one of Kelly's ACT workshops in Houston, Texas, in 2006 (looking back on this now, he recalls only going to Kelly's workshop because the one led by Kelly's mentor, Steve Hayes, was full). This meeting eventually resulted in their collaboration on *Mindfulness for Two*, a book for professionals that offers an ACT approach to the fostering of mindfulness in psychotherapy. That book is written in Kelly's voice. In writing *Things Might Go Terribly, Horribly Wrong*, though, we found our voices a little harder to separate. As you read along, just assume that the "we" mentioned is both of us. Though Troy was the anxious wine salesman we talked about earlier in the chapter, in this book we share a common voice, and our chief concern is you and your experience with anxiety.

Who You Are

Time and space are not on our side when it comes to getting to know you, reader. You come to this text from a place and time we can only imagine. We have to do a little guessing in order to figure out anything about you, but we think there's value in doing so. If nothing else, our efforts might help you figure out what you're getting yourself into by reading this book.

We assume that you're at least somewhat concerned about the role anxiety plays in your life or the life of someone you care about. We assume, since you've chosen to read up on the subject, you're willing to do at least a little work in the service of changing your life for the better. We assume that you've tried, by whatever means, to get rid of anxiety in the past without success or with limited success, and you're willing to give something new a try. And, finally, we assume that you're willing to tolerate the possibility that, in the course of doing this work, you won't get rid of anxiety, avoid it, push it away, or remove it from your experience. We'll take for granted that you've paid some cost because of anxiety, that it has been for you, at least some of the time, a source of suffering and strife. We'll assume that, given the choice, you would elect to let go of that suffering and get on with your life—even if getting to that point might mean engaging with some things that are hard.

And what might that life look like? We think you're in a better position to know than we are. Maybe it would include moments of sweetness like embracing loved ones you could finally fly to visit. Or maybe it would include taking the subway across town to an art gallery despite the fact that you're not totally comfortable traveling underground. Or maybe it would look very much like your life now, except that you'd actually be able to get to sleep at night. All in all, we think the possibilities are endless.

Oh, and one more thing: while we'll do our best to get to the point from now on, we need to assume that you're curious by nature and won't mind taking the long way around to an idea every once in a while (because sometimes that's the best way to get there).

How to Use This Book

Well, read it.

We're not being flip. What we're getting at is that this isn't a typical self-help book. We hope you'll want to read it or savor it rather than "do" it, "work" in it, or "get through" it. Take your time. Meander or skip around. Don't rush. We promise: there's no surprise ending (at least, not one that you won't make for yourself).

This book is rather unusually focused on processes rather than outcomes. It won't help you manage or get rid of anxiety, teach you to stop negative thoughts, or assist you in avoiding pain. It will help you learn to live a little freer each day, to find just a little bit more space in your life to breathe and rest and live. You'll find little games scattered throughout the text, activities that we think will help you experience the ideas we're describing, but the approach here isn't necessarily stepwise or structured. The book, unavoidably, has a last page, but we sincerely hope you won't find the "end" of what we're discussing here anytime soon. Rather, we hope this collection of ideas, observations, and stories will stick with you like a good supper, nourishing you and giving you the wherewithal to move your life in a direction that you care about.

So, without further ado, let's get started. If you're willing to come with us on this journey, we think we can help you find your way to a life liberated from anxiety. We humbly invite you, and we'll be sincerely honored if you choose to join us.

2

Anxiety:
Form,
Function,
and the
Unity of
Suffering

Livia (could go off): Stop it, Junior, you're making me very upset!

Junior: I don't like to, Livia, but I'm all agita all the time. And I'll tell you something else. Things are down. All across the board.

—*The Sopranos,* "The Sopranos (pilot)" (Chase 2002)

So you're all agita all the time. You worry. You're afraid. Maybe you panic sometimes when there doesn't seem to be an obvious reason for alarm. You can't stop asking yourself the question, "What if...?" You can't shake the feeling that things might go terribly, horribly wrong. In short, you're anxious.

In this chapter, we'll start by looking briefly at the ways in which most people, including many professionals, such as psychologists and doctors, speak about the *form* of anxiety disorders. Then we'll move on to a different discussion, one about the *function* that anxiety fulfills in your life. And finally, we'll wrap up the chapter by considering the possibility that anxiety is just one point on the continuum of human suffering, that it might not differ all that much from the other problems we face in our lives. With the idea of "problems in living" in mind, we'll have the stage set for our discussion about how the conversation we'll have in this book can lead you to a richer and more purposeful life.

Labeling Anxiety Behavior

Let's start with something of a disclaimer here: we're not totally convinced of the value of the disorder diagnoses that follow. The labels that psychologists (and the rest of us) apply to certain general patterns of behavior are categories, ways of organizing and speaking about the world—and, as we'll see as we go along, ways of speaking, words, and the stories we tell ourselves and others can cause suffering and strife just as easily as they can overcome obstacles and solve the problems we encounter each day. Your efforts to shoehorn yourself into one or more of the following diagnostic jackets won't get you closer to living a life free from the constraints of anxiety, and it may make your suffering more acute. But, especially if you read a lot about anxiety, you're going to encounter these terms, so you might want to know what they refer to.

The descriptions and diagnostic criteria for these disorders are set down in a phone-book-sized volume called the *Diagnostic and Statistical Manual of Mental Disorders*, a book perhaps better known by its initials as the *DSM*. In its section on anxiety disorders, the *DSM* describes (American Psychiatric Association 2000) seven distinct diagnoses (and a few other related problems that qualify for behavior related to health problems, substance abuse, and so forth). Generally, you need to manifest a certain set of anxiety-related symptoms for a period of time—often six months—on more days than not in order for a professional to officially diagnose you with one of these disorders. The diagnoses are described next.

(But, one last time, we implore you! Hold what follows very lightly. We'll go into more detail about why a little later, but for now try to remember that applying labels to jars does nothing to change their contents. These are categories only, and there may be good reasons for you to be suspicious of them.)

Specific Phobia: How do you feel about heights, spiders, snakes, flying, and needles? If these are a few of your favorite things, you're a pretty unusual person. Most of us have some stuff that gives us the creeps, but if you tend to feel extreme fear in the presence of certain objects or situations and go to extraordinary lengths to avoid these same, you might be said to have a *specific phobia*. Taken as a group, specific phobias are the most common of the anxiety disorders, with some studies suggesting that about 9 percent of the adult American population suffers from a phobia in any given year (Kessler et al. 2005). And the specific phobias, especially the uncommon ones, have really cool names that many of us (unless we suffer from logophobia, a fear of words) love to memorize: acrophobia (heights), aichmophobia (needles), bufonophobia (toads), and so forth.

In order for your fear to be officially labeled a phobia, it needs to actually bother you. Depending on the circumstances of your life, you can be said to have a certain fear, even a very strong one, that has relatively little influence on your life. If you can live fully and richly without ever setting foot on an airplane, going near an airport, or living beneath a flight path, even a complete and consuming fear of flying might not be much of a problem for you. But phobias can exact a high cost if they stand between you and things you want. If advancing in your career or spending precious time with people you love depends on air travel, that same fear of flying might be crippling.

Social Phobia: One intense fear that's distinguished from the specific phobias is the fear of embarrassment and humiliation in front of others, known as *social anxiety disorder* or *social phobia*. This condition is very common, with about 7 percent of the adult American population experiencing diagnosable levels in any given year (ibid.). This statistic leaves out the countless individuals who typically feel shy, uncomfortable, and ill at ease in social situations *without* meeting all of the specific diagnostic criteria for clinical social phobia, making this sort of problem very common indeed. For those said to have social phobia, parties, gatherings, meetings, and public-speaking responsibilities can be the source of considerable anxiety. Often, these folks respond to this anxiety by going to great lengths to avoid the situations (or the threat of the situations) that trigger it. Given that we're social creatures by nature and that social contact is more or less ubiquitous in our daily lives, this problem, unlike specific phobias, generally can't come up in a person's life without significant consequences.

Agoraphobia: Another variety of intense fear that's recorded separately from the larger group of specific phobias is *agoraphobia*, which is described as a fear of having a panic attack (see below) in a situation in which escape wouldn't be possible, help wouldn't be available, or embarrassment would be unavoidable. This fear tends to lead sufferers to avoid open or public spaces. The *DSM* distinguishes between agoraphobia connected to a history of panic disorder and the same condition in people without such a history. Agoraphobia is relatively rare, affecting only .8 percent of American adults in a given year (ibid.).

Panic Attacks and Panic Disorder: If, seemingly out of the blue, you're overcome by a wave of severe anxiety that results in physical symptoms such as hyperventilation, a racing heart, nausea, a choking sensation—the list is very long—you're likely experiencing a *panic attack*. If you have recurrent panic attacks without any obvious cause and you spend a considerable amount of time worrying or thinking about your panic attacks, you might be said to have *panic disorder*. One common response to a persistent pattern of panic attacks is agoraphobia; it's so common, in fact, that the two conditions are often discussed together. Panic is sometimes distinguished from other forms of anxiety by the mysterious nature of its triggers. Somewhat less than 3 percent of the adult American population will suffer from panic disorder in a given year (ibid.). It stands to reason that the number of people who experience isolated or less frequent panic attacks is far greater.

Acute Stress Disorder: *Acute stress disorder* is unusual among the anxiety diagnoses in the *DSM* in that, by diagnostic definition, it will go away in a month—or, rather, it will either go away or transform into a chronic condition that will, at that point, cease to be acute stress disorder. This condition arises as the result of an experience that involves either the real or perceived threat of death or serious injury to the eventual sufferer or to others, as well as feelings of helplessness, fear, and horror on the part of the sufferer. Common situations that might meet these conditions are accidents; natural disasters; violent crimes such as robbery, murder, or rape; and exposure to combat situations. To be diagnosed with acute stress disorder, the sufferer must feel several symptoms after, and as a direct result of, the distressing experience. These may include a pervasive numbness, a sense that the world is unreal, a sense that the sufferer is somehow outside of his body, and a loss of memory of the traumatic event. He also must relive the experience in some way—dreams, flashbacks, ruminations, and so forth—and must persistently avoid exposure to situations and things that evoke the event. Finally, the sufferer must, well, suffer as a result of all of these things, feeling distressed or impaired in life as a result of the anxiety associated with the experience. Acute stress disorder often emerges almost immediately after the distressing event but, according to the diagnostic criteria, must begin within four weeks. In order to qualify for the diagnosis, the symptoms need to persist for at least two days and not more than one month, lest the acute stress disorder be relabeled as...

Post-Traumatic Stress Disorder (PTSD): The diagnostic criteria for *post-traumatic stress disorder* (PTSD) are more or less the same as those for acute stress disorder, except that the symptoms don't go away in a month. To be diagnosed with PTSD, you need to be exposed to an extreme situation in which the loss of life or severe injury either takes place or is a possibility for you or others proximate to you. You need to reexperience the events in some way, engage in active avoidance of things and situations that recall the event, and experience significant distress and disability in your life as a result. The anxiety symptoms associated with PTSD can be chronic, persisting for whole lifetimes in some cases. Research suggests that about 3 percent of American adults suffer from PTSD in a given year (ibid.), and we might reasonably assume that the percentage of acute stress disorder sufferers is similar or greater.

Obsessive-Compulsive Disorder (OCD): If you don't suffer from OCD, you might be familiar with it from depictions of the disorder in popular media, such as the TV shows *Monk* and *Curb Your Enthusiasm*. If OCD is part of your life, though, we suspect you won't easily find the humor in these characterizations of the problem. OCD is a spectrum of behaviors characterized by obsession with certain thoughts, often in alternation with compulsive behaviors intended to neutralize the obsessions. We say "often" here because psychologists have identified some varieties of OCD that are known as *pure obsessions*. People suffering with pure obsessions are beset with reoccurring, discomforting thoughts, often of a sexual, violent, or religious nature, but they don't engage in the overt compulsive behaviors found in other varieties. There's some debate about whether pure obsessions are really free from corresponding compulsions or involve covert mental compulsions intended to neutralize the obsessions. Common examples of OCD behavior that might include covert compulsions include an obsession with contamination or infection paired with a washing or cleaning compulsion, and an obsession with the possibility of a catastrophic fire or burglary combined with a compulsion to repeatedly check the knobs on the stove or the locks on the doors. A compulsive urge to hoard objects and animals, and an obsession with sin coupled with a compulsion to confess are other examples of OCD behavior.

OCD is relatively rare, affecting only 1 percent of the adult American population in a given year (ibid.).

Generalized Anxiety Disorder (GAD): GAD describes a pattern of frequent and excessive worry about events or situations. Someone with GAD is likely to report that she feels overwhelmed or stressed out about the possibility that things in her life might go terribly, horribly wrong, although she might not be able to point exactly to a specific situation that triggered her worry or to a specific bad outcome that she fears. Physical symptoms like heart palpitations, dizziness, restlessness, muscle tension, irritability, and lack of sleep are often mentioned in connection with GAD. Once again, Ronald Kessler and colleagues put the one-year prevalence of this disorder at about 3 percent of the adult American population. Interestingly, while specific phobias are the most common anxiety disorders in the general adult American population, among those over sixty years of age with pervasive anxiety disorders, GAD is the most commonly observed disorder, observed in some 11 percent of that population (Calleo and Stanley 2008).

Finding Function in Anxiety

So, did you recognize yourself in any of those diagnoses? No? Well, congratulations. You don't have a problem with anxiety.

Of course we're not being serious. Actually, it's more likely that you saw yourself in more than one, even if you regard your problems with anxiety as moderate. Categories are like that. To paraphrase the 1989 movie *Field of Dreams*: build them, and they will come. The human mind has a pronounced inclination to group things, to collect them into rows and columns, to draw boxes around them. The very act of designating diagnostic categories is a kind of engraved invitation to our minds to start putting people into them. But a label doesn't tell the whole story. Maybe it doesn't even tell some of the story.

What are these diagnostic labels, after all? Conceptually, they're the legacy left to the mental health profession from its history as an outgrowth of the medical profession. Remember that minds like to make categories, and remember also that minds like to fill categories once they've been created. In medicine, diagnostic categories seem to make some sense. If you turn up at your doctor's office complaining of a painful sore throat and swollen glands along with white spots on your tonsils, she can run a throat culture on you. If the culture detects the bacterium *Streptococcus pyogenes* in and around your throat, voila! You *have* strep throat, and your doctor can prescribe a course of antibiotics for you. If you come into the exam room complaining of pain and swelling in your arm after falling off a fence, an X-ray can usually confirm whether you *have* a broken radius bone, which your doctor can then set and cast for you.

With mental health problems like anxiety, though, we don't have the advantage of easily identifiable biological markers to look for to indicate whether someone *has* a problem. There's no test for the anxiety bacteria, virus, or gene—because, at least insofar as we know at this point, mental health problems like anxiety are not directly caused by any biological or genetic agents. So far as we know now, mental health problems appear to arise from the complicated interaction of cognitive, behavioral, biological, and environmental factors, the combination of which leads us to struggle in our lives. Because mental health problems do appear to be very complicated, they tend to defy classification when you look closely at them.

Consider acute stress disorder, which we described previously. Let's imagine someone who has witnessed a horrific car accident. He has trouble sleeping at night. When he tries to go about his day, he relives the accident, often in vivid daydreams that keep him nervous and distracted. Because he persistently avoids cars and highways, he loses his job and is unable to pick up his kids from school. Clearly he's suffering, but according to the diagnostic categories, he actually has a different disorder the first Friday after the accident than he does two months later, even if his behavior looks to any outside observer exactly the same from the first point in time until the second.

Mental health problems like anxiety are complicated; they manifest differently in different people, and they can incorporate a huge range of possible behaviors. This astonishing diversity makes it hard to speak about them categorically—at least in any very meaningful way. But if it's hard to talk about mental illness diagnoses, it's really hard to pin down what, exactly, is the normal, baseline quality of human mental health. It's not normal for a human being to have a big mess of *Streptococcus pyogenes* bacteria in his tonsils. Nor is it normal for him to have a fractured radius. But what's the "normal" amount of worry you should experience? How much fear is "appropriate" in a given situation?

What we're getting at here is that we might be missing something if we focus, as the diagnostic labels do, on the *form* of anxiety behavior. But form is only part of the story. To get a different perspective, let's take a look at what *function* anxiety might be fulfilling in your life.

Eluding Ambiguity

Before we go on, play a stupid little game with us.

Game: Two Be's or Not Two Be's
Props: Your copy of *Things Might Go Terribly,
Horribly Wrong* • **Difficulty:** Easy

Before you start playing this game, make a little promise to
yourself: commit to playing this game for at least two minutes
after you read and understand the rules.

The objective of this game is to determine conclusively
whether the word "be" occurs twice and only twice on the
very first line of text on page 104 of this book. There's no
time limit to the game, and there are only three rules: First,
you must not, at this moment, know for certain whether
there are two be's on the first line of page 104. Who knows?
Maybe you're the kind of reader who skips around a lot and
is very observant of small details. Second, you mustn't, by any
means whatsoever, look at, scan, examine, turn to, or otherwise investigate what's printed on page 104. Neither may you
ask anyone to do it for you or to reveal their prior knowledge
of what's printed on the page, nor may you use any kind of
device to record the information for you to review later. And,
no, you mayn't hold page 103 up to a bright light and read
through the other side. Third, you can't guess, just to get the
whole business over with.

We suggest a time limit of two minutes, but you can play
longer if you feel like it.

Oh, one more thing: during game play, try to pay attention to the thoughts that pop into your head and the sensations that you feel in your body. These will matter to our
discussion a little later.

Well, how'd it go? We said it was a stupid game—stupid in the
sense, at least, that it's not really a game at all. What the game does
is challenge you to find the conclusive answer to a yes-or-no question under conditions in which you simply cannot find the answer.
In other words, the game thrusts you into a very basic ambiguous

situation. In still other words, the game replicates in overly simplified miniature a great many of the situations that you face in your life—and all of the situations about which you will ever feel anxious.

You really wanted to look, didn't you? At first, you might have felt stoic about the whole thing. "I just can't win this game. I'll just sit here for two minutes and then move on." But human brains don't like ambiguity—and those of us who are prone to great suffering from anxiety *really* don't like it. And it turns out that there are pretty good reasons for not liking it—or, at least, there were at one time.

The Bear and the Blueberries

If your house burns down or you lose your life savings in a stock market crash, you're likely to be pretty upset. But you could also be out of sorts if your house *might* burn down or your finances *might* take a turn for the worse. We not only suffer when things *actually* go terribly, horribly wrong, but we also suffer when they *might* go wrong. In fact, we often prefer predictable, obvious suffering to suffering that may or may not happen at any given time. And there doesn't appear to be anything exclusively human about this.

A fair amount of basic behavioral research on nonhumans suggests that our furry friends prefer environments in which painful things are predictable over environments where they are not (Abbott 1985; Badia, Harsh, and Abbott 1979). Wire the floor of a rat's cage to shock it. Then, install a lever that, if pressed, will switch the shocks from coming at random times to coming at predictable intervals. You'll find that the rats predictably press the lever to produce regularly timed and predictable shocks. They'll predictably do this even when the absolute number, duration, and intensity of shocks are identical between the two shock modes.

Human beings share this preference for the predictable and unambiguous. It's not hard to imagine why this might be so. There are lots of ways for a species to survive. Let's say you're a frog. When you're ready to start a family, you'll either lay or fertilize thousands of eggs, because it's overwhelmingly the case that the vast majority of your offspring will be preyed upon by other organisms or will die before they reach maturity. Your life cycle is adapted for that kind of thing, so if a couple of thousand of your kids get eaten, the survival of your genes isn't especially threatened. But our human life cycle isn't adapted like a frog's. We have our babies one at a time or, more rarely, in twos or threes. We gestate them for nine months, and as a result, childbirth tends to be a pretty dramatic event for our species. Our offspring tend to be pretty helpless for something like five to seven years, and they don't reach sexual maturity for something in the neighborhood of thirteen years. From an evolutionary perspective at least, if even one of your kids gets eaten, it's not going to be the high point of your day. It takes a lot of work to get a human kid brung up and out of the house. The future of your genes hangs heavily on every one of your offspring. So for us, as for all creatures with relatively low reproductive rates, characteristics that lead to the survival of the individual organism are at a premium.

Let's look at the relationship between ambiguity and survival in our often hostile and dangerous world. Imagine two cavemen out on the savanna. They see a vague shape off on the horizon.

"Is that a bear or a blueberry bush?" the first asks.

"I think it's a blueberry bush," the second replies.

A little tentatively, the first says, "I don't know. It might be a bear."

"No, I really think it *is* a blueberry bush."

"Well, I'm going back in the cave, just in case."

The second caveman shrugs and dashes off into the distance. Later, he comes back to the cave, belly distended, talking endlessly about how fabulous the blueberries were. "They were the biggest, juiciest blueberries you've ever seen!" he cries. "I can hardly move, I'm so stuffed!"

That night the first caveman goes to bed a little unhappy and a little hungry. Imagine that this scenario plays out several times. Each time, the first one expresses his concern that the vague shape might be a bear and goes back to the cave, and each time, the second one expresses his equally strong conviction that the apparition is another blueberry heaven, just like last time.

And one time, after this exchange takes place, the second caveman goes swanning off toward the horizon with a blueberry basket on his arm. Only this time, he doesn't come back to the cave anytime soon. Night eventually falls, and in the morning, there's still no sign of our blueberry-loving friend. He might wait a little longer, but eventually the first caveman, the one who has missed more than a few blueberry lunches, gets up and goes over to the other part of the cave, where he gathers up the other caveman's stone ax, his mammoth hide, and, most importantly, his mate.

Our ancient ancestors were doubtless confronted with situations rather like the game you played at the beginning of the chapter: situations where something was or wasn't the case, in which there was no reliable way to tell the difference. The shape on the horizon was either a bear or a blueberry bush, and the only way to find out was to go and see for yourself. If you go off toward the vague shape often enough, eventually it turns out to be a bear, and that day you're the bear's lunch.

Now, if we were some kind of fantastical frog creatures that spawned thousands of young, we'd be in a very different position than the one we find ourselves in: "Hey, Junior #23,423, go see what that thing on the horizon is!" But we're not. In order for our genes to keep moving down the line, we need to live a relatively long time. For us, the central evolutionary imperative is that it's better to miss lunch than to *be* lunch. We're capable of missing lunch many, many times, but we can only *be* lunch once (and after that, maybe dinner and breakfast, but that's largely up to the bear).

We're the children of the children of the children (and so forth) of the ones who played it safe and went back to the cave. As we evolved for millions of years in an unforgiving world, natural selection weeded out the brazen and the brash. Our ancestors, the ones who survived and passed on the genetic material of which we are all made, were selected for their caution. They were the ones who assumed that what's bad is bad and what's ambiguous is bad too.

If you're visually inclined, the options look like this:

	It's a blueberry bush.	It's a bear.
I bet it's a blueberry bush.	I get lunch.	I am lunch.
I bet it's a bear.	I miss lunch (and survive).	I miss being lunch (and survive).

As a result, human beings generally experience ambiguity itself as unpleasant, something to be resolved quickly when possible, avoided when not. And for those of us who struggle with anxiety, ambiguity can be a source of considerable suffering. And we can go to incredible lengths to avoid it—even when we know intellectually that those lengths are causing us considerable harm. (Actually, we should mention that there's some flexibility in all of this. Of course, an organism that was *totally* averse to ambiguity would have disadvantages on par with those of us who are not averse to it at all. While the latter would go loping off to be eaten by bears, the former would starve to death in the small clearing in front of his cave. And even the most anxious among us can pretty well tolerate ambiguity in some areas. We're really speaking in generalities here.)

Consider someone who is addicted to heroin but is trying to clean up and stop using the drug. From the moment she decides to stop using, she finds herself in the middle of a very ambiguous situation. Will she stay clean, or will she use again? Will she? Won't she?

And the answer? No one knows. It's just like the game earlier in the chapter, only you can't cheat and look ahead. The person with the addiction doesn't have a crystal ball; she can't see the future. There's only one way to know for certain, only one way she can eliminate that dense ambiguity, and that's to stick that needle in her arm. In the moment she uses, she gets a moment of relief from the ambiguity. And, altogether too often, that moment is enough. It's almost not worth considering whether she knows or doesn't know that drug

31

use is harming her, draining her life of possibilities with each use. It's enough to realize that, for all of us some of the time—and some of us all of the time—the pain of not knowing can outweigh the pain of even the most destructive actions.

Game: Sitting Inside Significant Questions
Props: None • **Difficulty:** Hard

The silly game at the beginning of this chapter was just a warm-up. Here's the real thing. You see, ambiguity doesn't only present a problem for people wrestling with drug addiction. Consider some things in your own life around which you've felt anxiety about making a choice. Especially consider things with fairly high stakes that have left you worried: should you get married or divorced, have children, change careers, or start a new business? If your particular experience with anxiety is less tied to specific outcomes, you can play the game too. Imagine a situation in which you've felt anxious. Maybe you felt panicked as you tried to merge onto the freeway or when you stepped into the elevator; perhaps you were anxious about coming in contact with a dirty doorknob or handrail. In these cases, imagine where you were just before you started to feel anxious. Picture the moment before you turned onto the on-ramp, the time you spent waiting for the elevator to arrive, the walk you took toward the door or the stairs where you felt concern about getting contaminated.

Ponder one of these situations or another that feels significant to you. Try doing this while intentionally not deciding one way or the other, and without evaluating or drawing any conclusion. Will you make a particular decision? Will you enter into the situation in which you feel so anxious? Rather than decide or conclude, let yourself wonder what you will do.

If you notice yourself deciding or weighing the pluses and minuses, gently let go of that process and come back to the question. Repeat the question gently to yourself, listening with care to each word. If you find yourself concluding, "Well, I'm not really going to do that" or "Sure, that's a good idea," let yourself notice that you are drawing conclusions about an unknown future. Your conclusion may indeed be the most likely outcome, but sometimes very unlikely things happen. As many times as you find yourself concluding or deciding, gently come back to the question and linger. Let yourself wonder for a few minutes. Notice also how quickly you're ready to move on to the next thing on your to-do list.

The objective of this game is not *exposure*, a popular approach in therapy that works to reduce anxious feelings, although sometimes the game has some flavor of exposure work. The object is, rather, to come to develop sensitivity to the ways your mind and body react to ambiguous situations and to cultivate flexibility in the presence of that ambiguity. What do you find yourself doing? Rushing? Running? Arguing with yourself or tuning out? Learning to sit with ambiguity can be a very important start at a life liberated from anxiety—and the way to do it is to resist the urge to chase answers to questions that may actually be unanswerable.

An Alternative: Appreciating Ambiguity

Most of the things in life you truly care about are likely to be very ambiguous, and if you can't foster some ability to make a place for ambiguity, you're likely to be doomed to act in the service of its elimination—which is really a fancy and roundabout way of saying that you'll feel and suffer from anxiety much of the time.

Learning to love ambiguity can be a very powerful, if rather counterintuitive, act. By love here, we're not talking about falling in love or being in love. We mean love as an act. You can learn to care for and cherish ambiguity. You can invite it into your house for a while, give it a glass of lemonade, talk with it, and listen to what it has to say to you. You'll often find things in the midst of ambiguity that you can't see or experience anywhere else. This is a kind of out-there idea, one that's better expressed in poetry than in expository writing. As ever with poetry though, you might have to spend some quality time with the idea before it starts to speak to you:

> *At the still point of the turning world. Neither flesh nor fleshless;*
> *Neither from nor towards; at the still point, there the dance is,*
> *But neither arrest nor movement. And do not call it fixity,*
> *Where past and future are gathered.*
> *Neither movement from nor towards,*
> *Neither ascent nor decline.*
> *Except for the point, the still point,*
> *There would be no dance, and there is only the dance.*

> —T. S. Eliot, "Burnt Norton"

For the time being, though, let's just linger inside this issue of ambiguity. We've talked a lot about it, and some of what we've said might be resonating with you. But there's no need to "fix" it, now or even anytime soon. There's something very elemental about our lack of ease with ambiguity that we can't just wish or work away. And besides, your relation to the ambiguous is just part of the story of why you struggle with anxiety and how you can break free. Later in the book, when we start to talk about the process areas and how you can work within them, you'll find some more interesting things about how you approach ambiguity. In the meantime, let's consider another important function that anxiety might play in your life: problem solving.

The Problem with Problem Solving

Wherever you find a human, you find a problem. A simple breathing meditation provides a marvelous example of the near impossibility of separating humans from their problem solving, and it gives us a clear window through which to observe the human condition.

Game: Solving the Problem of Solving
the Problem of Solving the Problem of…
Props: None • **Difficulty:** Easy—or really,
really hard

You have everything you need to try this exercise. You know how to breathe. You know how to count to ten. You know how to sit. Play this game when you have a bit of time on your hands without any pressing responsibilities.

Sit down in a comfortable position. Gently close your eyes. Begin to count your breaths from one to ten, starting again when you reach ten. Then, watch the show.

Okay. Here I go: one, two—ow, my back hurts a little.

You adjust a little and solve the back-hurting problem.

Ah, that's better. One, two, three—gee, my knee hurts a little.

You move your knee a little bit and solve the knee-hurting problem.

There we go. Much better. Now I'm ready. One, two, three, four—this is going pretty well; feels nice—oops! Where was I?

Then you solve the wandering-mind problem—and so forth. As you go, notice how effortlessly your mind moves to solve problems and even invents problems for you to solve if none readily presents itself.

Give a human an altogether simple task and she'll somehow turn it into a problem to be solved. It's pretty much a given that if you have a pulse, you have a problem. And if you don't, give it a minute. The human capacity for problem solving seems near limitless. Of course, you get little reprieves here and there. But if it were common or easy to let go of problem solving, there wouldn't be a hundred meditative traditions to teach you the altogether simple skill of repeating a word or phrase, sitting, or breathing—of taking a moment to not problem solve.

The Blessing and the Curse of Problem Solving

As was the case with ambiguity, there are very good evolutionary reasons why problem solving is so essential to our nature. Let's go back to the ancient savanna for another minute. Imagine two new cavemen out in the grass on a warm summer day. One is a problem solver, like us. The other has a genetic predisposition to meditate, to drop out of the problem-solving mode of mind for long periods. The first guy is agitated, jumpy, and worrisome. His skin is bad; he has always got a frown on his face. He's concerned about his rumbling stomach and those growling sounds he started hearing in the cave last night. He gets up out of his clump of grass and starts wandering around the area, looking for a nest of grubs or a few pieces of fruit. Maybe he climbs a hill and looks out for a saber-toothed tiger on the prowl. All the while the second guy sits cross-legged under a tree counting his breaths. He's happy, well-adjusted, and popular at cave parties.

We probably don't need to follow this story out to its predictable (and probably gory) conclusion. If our two cavemen hear a lion roar while both are lingering out in a clearing, how they react will have a lot to do with whether their genes get passed on to future generations. The first one hears the roar and bolts, single-mindedly, to the hole in the rocks. The second starts to run but stops to notice the sensation of the grass beneath his feet, the cool breeze on his face, the inflow and outflow of his breath, and—chomp, chomp, chomp. In an environment where your basic survival is a struggle, where food is scarce, and where, for a lot of bigger and stronger creatures, you *are* the food, the dominance of the problem-solving trait is probably a very good thing.

So here we sit at the tip of an evolutionary branch, the ever-so-many great grandchildren of the grumpy and jumpy cave person, ready to find and solve any and every problem that exists now, existed in the past, or might exist in the future. The good news is that this inclination has made us the virtually undisputed masters of our universe. It has allowed us to outstrip every species on the planet in terms of our ability to spread across the face of the earth (and even off of it).

But the bad news is that this marvelous capacity hasn't come without a cost. The cost is that our urge to seek and solve problems isn't something we can easily turn on and off, and in our current environment, where most of the "threats" we face are psychological in nature (or, at the very least, aren't easily defended against using normal problem-solving means), this can become a real drag on our ability to live life in a valued and purposeful way. We spend a lot of time trying to solve problems that are essentially unsolvable. The irony is that, even in these situations, our problem-solving efforts *seem* to be in the service of getting us where we want to go. Have you ever made a little personal resolution to "once and for all" get a handle on your tendency to worry all the time? "That's it! I'm not going to spend every moment of my free time worrying about..." And then you set about to "solve" your worry problem. How did that work for you? Chances are, not so well.

The problem with problems is that when we're in the midst of problem solving, the rest of the world disappears for us. It makes sense that problems would dominate our awareness in this way.

The Caveman and the Hidey-Hole

Let's go back to the problem-solving caveman we were getting to know a few paragraphs back, the grumpy one. Imagine for a minute that today was a better day for him than most, and he's lying out on the grass in a sunny spot with a bellyful of food. He feels the soft grass pressing into his back, looks up at the clear blue sky, smells the sweet summer air, and feels the warmth of the sun on his face.

And then, all of a sudden, that saber-toothed tiger he was worrying about a few pages back starts to roar. What happens to his awareness of the grass, the scents in the air, the blue of the sky, the warmth of the sun? Gone. In that instant, everything vanishes from his awareness except the tiger and the best way to make it safely to a nearby hole in the rocks, the hole he knows about that's just a little smaller than the tiger and a little deeper than the tiger's paw can reach. The cat and the hidey-hole are the only things that matter to our caveman friend in that moment. The good news is that this single-minded attention to problem solving made it so his genes got passed on time and time again, eventually making it possible for you to buy and read this book.

The bad news is that, in this age of relative safety and abundance, many of the problems we encounter, which feel every bit as threatening to us as a hungry saber-toothed tiger, are, in fact, very different in kind from a hungry beast. What happens if you linger with a saber-toothed tiger? You get eaten. What happens, though, if you linger with worry, fear, or panic?

You might be tempted to say, "I'll get eaten metaphorically. I'd be pulled in, and my feelings of anxiety will get worse." Maybe yes, maybe no—and we'll have more to say about that later. But would you be willing to agree that there's a significant difference—a difference you could describe, document, take a picture of—between being eaten figuratively and being eaten in fact? If you can agree to only that much, then you might be willing to at least entertain, even briefly, the idea that a *possible* reaction to an anxiety-provoking situation might be to *not* run as fast from it as possible.

What if problem solving twenty-four hours a day, seven days a week isn't the best way to live? What if problem solving twenty-four hours a day, seven days a week isn't even the best way to solve most of our problems?

An Alternative: Math Problems and Sunsets

Well, if you don't solve your "problems in living," such as your problem with anxiety, what do you do with them? They sure as hell don't seem to be going away on their own.

Maybe you could try appreciating them. This is one of those things we'll have more to say about later, in chapter 8, which deals with the self-as-context process area, but it bears mentioning now: Anxiety is something that happens in your life. It's a part of your experience. It shapes you; how could it not? What would it be like if you just spent some time appreciating, gently, the subtle and not so subtle features of this force that molds you?

You're going to relate to some of the things in your life as if they were math problems. You'll try to figure them out. If they're hard, you'll struggle with them for a while. In some cases, they'll be too hard, and you'll give up on them and walk away. But some of the things in your life don't fit the mold of math problems, do they? What about your struggle with anxiety? Have you been able to figure out the answer to it? No matter how hard you struggled? You might have wanted to give up on it and walk away, but it's not so easy to walk away from problems that originate inside your head, is it? And what about the people in your life? Do they need to be solved? Have you ever been somebody's problem to be solved? In fact, maybe you know people who see you come into a room and know you're anxious. Perhaps you notice that they start treating you a little differently. When they see you enter a room, do they see you—the anxious person? And are they happy to see you? Or are you their problem to be solved? And how does that feel?

We like to think of sunsets as the opposite of math problems. What do you do with a sunset? You appreciate it. You sit on the beach and gaze in wonder that anything like that could have ever come to be. It's as big as day and free for everyone to look at. Do you know what makes a sunset a sunset? Sunlight refracting through dust and soot, and solid and liquid aerosols in the atmosphere is the correct answer, but it's not one that really does much justice to a blaze of orange and red filling up the evening sky.

What would it be like if you could learn to appreciate your feelings of anxiety? Sit with them? Get to know them? What would it be like if you could slow down enough to hear something different in a moment of anxiety than you've ever heard before? What if you could learn something from that moment that might inspire you to be kinder to yourself? To someone you love? To someone you barely know? What if something you learned from sitting and appreciating your anxiety for a moment might incline you to be kind to someone you really can't stand? How do you suppose that would change your life?

One of the really surprising things about climbing up inside our problems with living, making the choice to appreciate them, and

seeing what's really going on inside of them is that doing so tends to blur the distinctions we typically see when we think about our problems. Just like those diagnostic labels from the *DSM*, our own categorizing and labeling efforts can leave us with a pretty unworkable picture of the world. In the end, it turns out, all suffering seems to be of the same family.

> HORATIO: O day and night, but this is wondrous strange!
>
> HAMLET: And therefore as a stranger give it welcome.
>
> There are more things in heaven and earth, Horatio,
>
> Than are dreamt of in your philosophy.
>
> —Shakespeare, Hamlet, Act I, Scene V

The Great Fact of Human Suffering

One of the chief problems with a categorical way of thinking about anxiety is that it suggests a real difference in kind between, say, someone with agoraphobia and someone with generalized anxiety disorder. You can have one or the other. Maybe you can have both. But the categories we impose on this subject imply a useful distinction between one condition and the other. Is there really?

And if you push that question a little further, you might begin to wonder whether there's actually a useful distinction to be made between "having" an anxiety disorder and "not having" one. There's no question that most of us think about anxiety in terms of "having" or "not having" it, but how close is this way of seeing the world to our actual experience of it?

It's a question that deserves some attention. When you dig around inside it a little, you're likely to discover that there's a lot more similarities between our problems in living than differences, and this matters if you're looking to set yourself free from anxiety. In the

pages that follow, we're going to look at some numbers and observations that suggest a thread of suffering that runs throughout the cloth of human experience. Some of these observations might seem scary at first, and confronted with the pervasiveness of human suffering, you might be inclined to worry even more. So we'll tell you up front that the goal of this section is to help you see that all of us share a common fate in suffering. We think that the acceptance of that common fate is an important first step in finding our way to freedom in this life. And, in the latter chapters of the book that deal with the six ACT processes, we'll have a lot more to say about how to make that happen.

> The rejection of our common fate
>
> Makes us strangers to each other.
>
> The election of this common fate, in love,
>
> reveals us as one body.
>
> —Sebastian Moore

Think back on the prevalence numbers we cited as we described the various diagnostic labels psychologists give to anxiety disorders. The most prevalent diagnosis in the American adult population was specific phobia, at about 9 percent. Agoraphobia was the least prevalent in the same group, affecting only about .8 percent.

Now, unless you work in the psychology profession, the odds are that you're not terribly interested in finer points of mental disorder prevalence research. But if you have a history of struggle with anxiety—and particularly if you've been diagnosed and treated for an anxiety disorder—you might be interested in how common your experiences are when compared to the general public. And even if you think of your problems with anxiety as moderate or minor, you still might be interested in how statistics about mental illness come together to suggest something about our baseline state of mental health.

Numbers Can Be Misleading

It turns out that statements made about the prevalence of particular psychiatric diagnoses can be misleading. Taken one at a time, specific mental health diagnoses, such as the anxiety disorders we described earlier in this chapter, are relatively rare. If we widen our scope a little to include other diagnoses than just anxiety disorders and if we continue to look at the population of American adults, statistical research tells us to expect only about 3 percent to be diagnosable with drug dependence, another some 3 percent with generalized anxiety disorder, and another some 2.5 percent with chronic moderate depression, or dysthymia, within a given twelve-month period (Kessler et al. 1994).

All in all, they sound pretty rare, don't they? There's a certain safety in the rareness of these categories. The fact that the diagnoses are fairly uncommon puts a bit of distance between us and the suffering they represent, between our loved ones and that suffering. The categories are somewhat abstract and impersonal, which further removes them from an intimate connection to our experience. Even if you find yourself squarely within one of these diagnostic labels, one look at the numbers will remind you that you are in the minority, a very select club.

And most of the rest of the people you see each day are making it just fine, right? Let's look further into the numbers. Set aside these individual labels for a moment, and we see a much different picture. In the study we're citing above, Kessler and colleagues are collecting survey information for only 14 of the categories in the *DSM*. (There are, in fact, more than 150.) They report that more than 29 percent of fifteen- to fifty-four-year-olds experienced sufficient symptoms within the last twelve months to qualify for at least one of these fourteen clinical diagnoses.

Yet when you look a little deeper into the data, you find that, among fifteen- to twenty-four-year-olds, the rate was 34 percent. Keep in mind that the population Kessler and his colleagues are reporting wasn't selected because it was at risk for developing mental health problems. The researchers were simply looking at the adult American population at large.

We'll say that again just to make it clear: In one year, nearly a third of all American adults and more than a third of young adults experienced symptoms that were sufficient to diagnose a mental health disorder—one in three.

And if you find that number surprising, realize that it tells only a partial story about the scope of human suffering. Recall that Kessler and his colleagues were only reporting on clinical disorders, the so-called Axis I disorders that appear in the *DSM*—the kinds of mental health problems that you're probably most familiar with: anxiety, depression, eating disorders, and so forth. These figures don't include the dozens of other diagnoses that fall onto the other axes: conditions that are due to a pervasive psychological condition or personality disorder, those caused by medical conditions and brain injury, those that are directly tied to environmental conditions, and so forth.

These statistics also don't include subclinical cases, those in which an individual experiences the symptoms of a mental health disorder yet not often enough or extensively enough to actually be diagnosed by a professional. Imagine here a person who feels anxious more days than not, who has trouble controlling her worry, who experiences significant impairment at work and as she goes about living her life—but who nevertheless experiences fewer than the "required" number of symptoms, according to the *DSM*, for a formal diagnosis. Even if you're not a trained psychologist, does it seem intuitively true to you that there could be any difference in kind between someone who has two and someone who has three of, say, six symptoms?

And the figures also don't tell us how many people live their lives under a cloud of worry or the threat of panic but either don't meet the criteria for diagnosis or never seek treatment at all. They don't tell us about the people who live in broken, loveless, or silent marriages or the ones who are isolated and lonely. They don't tell us whether this person finds her work meaningless or if that one can't talk to his children.

Game: Taking in the Scope of Suffering
Props: The world • **Difficulty:** Hard

The objective of this game is to help you see the problems you have with living, including anxiety, in the greater context of the people you interact with every day. Once you read the rules and understand the concept, take them with you on a normal work or weekend day.

As you head out in the morning, silently notice the people you encounter throughout the day. Let your attention move from one face to the next as you walk down the street. Count people silently as you meet them: one, two, three; one, two, three. Let yourself notice that approximately every third person could be diagnosed with a mental health disorder this year if only the right set of questions were asked of him. Don't try to imagine what it would be, and don't try to decide which of the people you encounter would be the ones. Instead, try to get a feeling for the breadth and reach of these problems in living, the real vastness of human suffering. Notice also that, for the most part, everyone you're likely to meet in the course of your day as you silently play this game will look just fine.

Going to Extremes

The fact of suicide and research into the frequency with which people have serious thoughts about suicide paint another picture of the scope of human suffering. Even more so than the mental health diagnoses we've discussed, suicide itself is relatively rare. In the United States each year, there are approximately eleven deaths by suicide per hundred thousand people. In other words, about .01 percent of the population will die by suicide in any given year (Centers for Disease Control and Prevention, n.d.), and by any measure, this makes actual suicide a decidedly uncommon phenomenon. But one study (Chiles and Strosahl 2005) found that 20 percent of a statistically relevant sample of American adults reported a two-week period at some time in their lives during which they gave serious thought to taking their own lives, which included making a plan and identifying the means for carrying out the deed. The study identified an additional 20 percent of the population who had given suicide serious consideration but who hadn't made a specific plan for the purpose. Taken together, these numbers suggest that nearly half the group was likely to suffer to such an extent that they seriously considered taking their own lives as a way to end their suffering. And we're inclined to imagine that this statistic could apply more broadly—much more broadly.

If it does, what might this mean for you? It might mean that half the people you know have had, or will have, a moment of such pain and despair that death seems a kinder option than soldiering on. But will they tell you? No. Neither half nor likely even one in a hundred will ever say a word. They'll come to work, to class, to the dinner table. You'll ask them how they are, and they'll tell you they're fine.

Like anxiety disorders, suicide seems pretty safe when we view it as an obscure statistic. But really consider the implications of nearly half of us giving serious thought to self-slaughter. Let yourself recognize whom this is about. As you move through your day, pause for just a moment as you greet each person and count silently again: one, two; one, two; one, two. Let yourself hesitate and glance a moment and look into those eyes. Let yourself wonder. Don't do anything about it. Just pause and wonder. At the next staff meeting, cocktail party, or PTA social, let your eyes move about the room. Let it sink in that nearly half of those you see will know this dark night of the soul. And, most likely, the next day they'll come into work, and they'll be "fine."

Even that is too abstract. How many brothers and sisters do you have? Stop a moment and close your eyes. See their faces, and let yourself quietly say their names as you do. Now count again. One, two; one, two. See if you can see, as you look into those eyes, hints of that suffering—just the other side of "fine."

Worse still—do you have children? One, two; one, two. See if you notice—right in this moment—how much you want us to stop, to move on to the next point. And, in that rejection, we find the altogether human reaction to suffering. We want to hold it distant or not at all. In that rejection, we also see the source of all that silence; we see why the automatic answer to "How are you?" is "Fine."

And how about you? Do you know that dark night? And how are you? And who knows about that?

Let's be clear: We're not suggesting that you go out and start proclaiming the fact of your suffering. This exercise of wondering how many of those we encounter each day suffer in silence is an act of appreciation, not a prescription for future action. And if you can start to appreciate the real scope of human suffering, that suffering of which your anxiety is an undeniable part, what are the implications for the way you will relate to the other people in your life? Consider it this way: conjure up the image of the person at your workplace whom you like the least. Imagine that you found out that this person has precisely the same difficulty you have. Imagine that, even though it doesn't look that way, it's true. You may still not like the person in the least, but see if knowing this about her wouldn't soften your regard for her. What are the implications for the ways in which you relate to yourself, the ways you engage with your experience of anxiety? What if your willingness to let this suffering come close to you allows you, maybe for the first time, to truly hear the heart of this suffering? Really, it's not even so much letting it come close as it is letting yourself see how close it already is.

Why Acknowledge Suffering?

We've suggested already that anxiety has at its core disquietude caused by ambiguity and a strong inclination toward problem solving. When we're faced with uncertainty, many of us regard it as a problem, and very often the solution to that problem is to get away fast. In light of what we've just said about the ubiquity of suffering, you'd think it would be pretty normal to want to avoid it when it's possible to do so. And this is quite true. It's entirely normal. And it's also normal for the dog that has been hit by a car to bite the stranger who tries to rescue it from the middle of the road. But the bite doesn't help the dog get to the veterinarian.

If the sources of suffering in your life had teeth and claws, if engagement with them came with the very real chance that you would become somebody's lunch, it would be both wise and constructive for you to withdraw from them. But what do you suppose are the consequences of withdrawing from psychological suffering—from worry, from the threat of embarrassment, from fear? What do you suppose is on the other side of these things?

Here's a hint: it's not a bear. It's nothing less than your life. If suffering is ubiquitous in life, the withdrawal from and avoidance of suffering is accordingly the withdrawal from and avoidance of life. You need not take this on faith. Check it out in your own experience. Has working at solving the anxiety problem brought you closer to people? Enriched your life? Think about a specific time when you worked really hard on solving the anxiety problem and see if that was when you felt most connected to others and to your own life. And given that suffering touches the lives of all of us, like Sebastian Moore suggests, the rejection of suffering divides us and keeps us apart. When you run away from suffering, you miss other things, rich and varied, that are inextricably linked to suffering.

The things we most want our lives to be about are intimately connected to the ways in which we suffer the most. Consider the ways you experience anxiety in your life and see if they aren't bound to something you care deeply about. Would you be worried about your performance on the job if being a successful and respected professional meant nothing to you? Would you stay in your house all day if it didn't matter to you whether you could maintain your self-control and composure in public? If you didn't care deeply about your own well-being or your ability to care for the people you love, would you be at all concerned about going down that jet ramp and getting onto that plane? (By the way, we'll have more to say about how our values and vulnerabilities are poured from the same vessel in chapter 6.)

Liberation: The Other Great Fact of Human Suffering

The one great fact of human suffering is that it lies all about us. We're capable of suffering under just about any condition. In the poem "Dover Beach," we hear the words of the newlywed listening to the waves break on the sea coast:

Ah, love, let us be true
To one another! for the world, which seems
To lie before us like a land of dreams,
So various, so beautiful, so new,
Hath really neither joy, nor love, nor light,
Nor certitude, nor peace, nor help for pain;
And we are here as on a darkling plain.

—Matthew Arnold, "Dover Beach"

Some honeymoon. We might imagine his wife abed and Matthew at the window, contemplating the darkness and futility of the world. Frustrated with his poetic melancholy, mightn't Mrs. Arnold say, "Just come to bed, dear"?

It appears to be possible for humans to suffer under any and all conditions. However, there's a complement to the extraordinary capacity of humans to suffer, and that's our equally remarkable capacity for liberation. An example can be found in Victor Frankl's landmark book *Man's Search for Meaning* (1959). In the book, Frankl describes his experience in the Nazi death camps during World War II. He speaks at length about suffering in the camps, which is no surprise. However, the point upon which the entire book turns is Frankl's description of the time he and a companion find a way to escape the camp. They gather some food and a few other supplies. The day before their planned escape, Frankl decides to make one last round of the patients in his makeshift hospital. He knows that his medical efforts are largely futile. The prisoners under his care are dying of malnutrition, dysentery, and untold other causes. He has little to offer them except comfort.

Frankl describes one fellow he had been particularly keen on saving but who was clearly dying. On Frankl's last round, the man looks into his eyes and says, "You, too, are getting out?"

Frankl writes, "I decided to take fate into my own hands for once." He tells his friend that he will stay in the camp and care for his patients. Upon returning to sit in the hospital ward, Frankl describes a sense of peace unlike any he has ever experienced.

What Frankl experienced that day in the camp was liberation. Even though his outward circumstances were some of the cruelest fetters devised by human beings, Frankl was able to experience freedom. And what we take away from his story is that no matter what circumstances you've suffered, no matter what costs you've paid or losses you've endured in connection to anxiety, it's possible for you to experience freedom and go on to live a rich and purposeful life. Frankl gives voice to something that we strongly believe to be true: one great fact of human suffering is that it's pervasive; the other great fact is that liberation is within our reach.

By this, of course, we don't mean liberation from pain. This isn't a "happily ever after" kind of a story, as you might have guessed from the Robert Burns epigraph that kicked off the book. What we do mean is that, in the middle of this ocean of suffering, there's a means available to us all to let go of our struggles and choose to move our lives in the direction of meaning and purpose—that we're all capable of having a life we can say yes to, independent of the pain it brings. And this, we believe, means that even if you've been struggling your whole life with worry, fear, panic—with anxiety in any of its forms— you can find a way through those experiences that will lead you to a life of your choosing.

In the next six chapters of the book, we'll explore some areas of your life—the six process areas that are central to ACT—to help you see some things you might do to make this vision into a reality.

3

A Fish
on Dry
Land:
Anxiety
in the
Present
Moment

Still thou art blest, compar'd wi' me
The present only toucheth thee:
But, Och! I backward cast my e'e.
On prospects drear!
An' forward, tho' I canna see,
I guess an' fear!*

—Robert Burns, "To a Mouse"

Here we go: another stanza from Burns's famous poem about a mouse, which turns out to be more and more relevant to our discussion of anxiety. In the epigraph to chapter 1, Burns observes that men and mice plans, no matter how well thought out they are, have an alarming tendency to not turn out as intended. And now, in the stanza above, Burns observes that, though they're in a similar strait as mice in the planning department, humans actually have it worse. Problems in "the present only" concern our four-footed friends, while we have to contend with both our memories of misfortunes past and the uncertain (and probably nasty) future that awaits us. Sound like anything else you might have read lately?

Take a look at the title of this book. Read it carefully, word by word. For a minute, we're going to get nitpicky about semantics. Pay special attention to the verb phrases. Notice that we chose to call the book *Things* Might Go *Terribly, Horribly Wrong*. Given our subject, another possible title might have been *Things* Have Gone *Terribly, Horribly Wrong*. (We never really considered this, because then it would be a book about recovering from catastrophe.) But the title

*Still, you are blessed, compared with me! / The present only touches you: / But oh! I backward cast my eye, / On dreary prospects! And forward, though I cannot see, / I guess and fear!

of the book couldn't possibly have been *Things* Are Going *Terribly, Horribly Wrong*—at least not if the book were going to be about anxiety—because anxiety is out of place in the present moment. It depends on the past and the future for its existence. This understanding matters if you hope to let go of your struggle with anxiety.

But don't take our word for it. Let's play a little game to get a feeling for what anxiety might look like if it were focused on the present moment.

Game: Being Anxious About Now
Props: Only your imagination
• **Difficulty:** Medium

Start by calling to mind something you feel anxious about or have felt anxious about in the last couple of days. It could be anything: the feeling that you're not doing well at work, concern that there won't be enough money at the end of the month to pay all the bills, a nagging doubt that the people you have lunch with really don't like you all that much.

Now sit with that thought for a minute and let it take shape in your mind. Let it be as detailed as you can. Notice not only the details of the thing that might go terribly, horribly wrong but also how it makes you feel. Does your stomach tighten? Does your heart beat faster? Really connect with what it feels like to be anxious.

Once you have a very clear image of the thing you're feeling anxious about in your mind and you've noted how it makes you feel, try to imagine that whatever it *is* is happening right here, right now. Imagine that whatever it is that you've felt uneasy about is staring you right in the face.

Let's say you were thinking about the possibility that the people you have lunch with really don't like you all that much. What would that look like? You're sitting in a café or a lunchroom. You're bantering with your usual cast of companions when one of them—let's call her Bernice—sets down

54

her ham sandwich and diet soda and looks you straight in the eye: "You know, I've never told you this before, but I really don't like you very much. Come to think of it, none of us does. All these years we've tolerated you in here at lunchtime just to keep the peace. But the truth is I really wish—and I think I speak for everyone at the table when I say this—that you would start eating at your desk instead of in here with the rest of us."

The other people at the table all nod their heads and murmur their assent. Bernice stands up and points her finger at the door.

Once you've imagined the thing you've felt anxious about actually happening, take a good, long look at yourself, at your mind and your body. Notice the thoughts coursing through your head. Describe your physical sensations to yourself as completely as you can.

Well, what did you notice? How was your experience of anxiety—of misfortune that *might* happen—different from your experience of misfortune *actually* happening? The little narrative we described in the example, in which you didn't feel good enough to be part of a group, describes a kind of anxiety that's familiar to a lot of people. Even if it doesn't happen to be something you get bothered about, let's pretend it is, for the sake of our discussion. We imagine that thinking about being at the lunch table, wondering whether your companions like you or not, brought up some typical anxiety symptoms: racing thoughts, an accelerated heart rate, a clammy feeling on your brow or palms. But when Bernice said her piece, the feel of the situation changed pretty quickly, didn't it? Instead of worrying that your lunch mates might not appreciate you, you got the message loud and clear. Gone was the sense of unease, of uncertainty, of nagging doubt. Or, if there was any anxiety, see if it wasn't connected to things in the past that had a bit of this flavor or worries about the future. More importantly maybe, gone was the ambiguity associated with the situation. Anxiety faded quickly, to be replaced, depending on your disposition, with either anger or a sense of being profoundly hurt. Bernice is a first-class jerk! Who talks to people that way?! If you found yourself in this situation, you might lash out, run away, or, at the very least, be dumbstruck. In any case, it's more than likely that you would feel and behave very differently while being anxious about the event than while in the middle of it.

Anxiety in the Moment Is Like a Fish on Dry Land

What we're driving at is that the things and situations about which we feel anxiety aren't anchored in the present moment. If we feel apprehension and alarm about something in the here and now, we don't refer to it as anxiety. Instead, we call it *fear*. When you think things *are going* terribly, horribly wrong, fear is what grips you. And, unlike anxiety, which strives to neutralize ambiguity and is only minimally useful in these days of more or less harmless threats, fear is generally pretty useful stuff.

If you hear shrieks and gunfire coming from the room at the end of the hall, you might decide to go the other way. If you're at the beach and you see a big dorsal fin cutting through the waves, you might put off going for a swim. If unproductive people in your office are getting fired left and right, you might take special care to meet all your deadlines and complete all your tasks. In all these cases, you're responding to something in the here and now in a way that might protect you from harm.

In addition to how you might respond to the threat of impending misfortune, there are still other ways you're likely to respond to things *actually* going terribly, horribly wrong—to situations where bad things are actively happening to you. And as you might imagine, these behaviors, being even more grounded in the present than fear responses, are even less like anxiety. These vary from automatic behaviors that your body initiates without any thought—as happens when you jerk your hand away from something hot—to reactions that you do think about first, such as pulling your car to the side of the road after you've been in a collision. In any case, the fact that you're reacting to some concrete event taking place in the present moment precludes your experience from being anxiety.

Now, just because you think there's something around you that might harm you doesn't mean there actually *is* something there for you to be afraid of. Just thinking that a threat is at hand is enough to make you feel fearful. But this conjured fear is still very unlike anxiety. It's predicated on the assumption of a real threat in the present moment. If someone were to ask you, "What are you afraid is happening right now?" you could give them an answer. Anxiety isn't like that; it needs to draw on the past or future to have any hold over you.

You can think of anxiety in the moment like a fish that's been chucked onto dry land. To flourish, a fish needs water over its gills and supporting its body. Anxiety, likewise, needs the murky past or mysterious future to feed it and keep it going. Without their respective natural environments to sustain them, both the fish and anxiety will quickly wither and expire. Realizing this is a huge step toward breaking the stranglehold anxiety can have on your life.

But how? Well, this is where our first ACT process comes in.

Contact with the Present Moment

From an ACT perspective, present-moment processes describe your ability to bring your attention to bear in a deliberate, focused, yet flexible way on the events of your life as they're unfolding in the here and now.

Think about how this contrasts with other kinds of focused attention that might not have the quality of flexibility. Have you watched a young person who's completely absorbed in a computer game? Sometimes she doesn't even blink. She's very focused on the unfolding of events on the computer screen, but the whole rest of the world could slip away during game play and she might just miss it. Or, if you have problems with flying, maybe you've passed the better part of the flight staring out the window at the wing, looking for evidence of fractures. In this case, you have the appearance of being focused on the present moment, but your attention is really directed at the imagined future (when the wing detaches from the fuselage and the plane pirouettes out of the sky in a ball of flame), and you probably aren't very flexible, either.

It's also possible to be connected to the present moment in a way that's very flexible but not very—wait! There's a bunny!—um, that is, in a way that's not very deliberate or focused. Being easily distracted by things that go on around you can demonstrate very flexible awareness of the present moment without demonstrating deliberate focus. Having a short attention span is a variety of this kind of process problem.

A number of mental health problems are deeply rooted in problems with maintaining contact with the present moment. The most striking is known as *dissociation*, a condition in which a person's environment has virtually no impact on him at all. But even less dramatic breakdowns in present-moment processes are very central to the experience of anxiety. Both worry and rumination are best understood as lapses in present-moment contact. When you worry, you lose contact with the present moment as you focus your attention on a conceptualized future. When you ruminate, it's more or less the same act, except that you focus on a conceptualized past.

> We can make our minds so like still water that beings gather about us, that they may see, it may be, their own images, and so live for a moment with a clearer, perhaps even with a fiercer, life because of our quiet.
>
> —W. B. Yeats, "New Chapters of Celtic Twilight, III"

(Remember when we mentioned in chapter 1 that each of these process areas could be reflected in the others? Here's an example you can check out for yourself when you get to the defusion discussion in the next chapter: You can think of worry and rumination as a lapse of contact with the present moment in that you become less sensitive to what's going on in the here and now. You can also think of the same worry and rumination as taking too literally your stories about the past and the future—and these are both examples of *fusion*.)

Live Life Where Anxiety Can't Thrive

So if anxiety can't really persist when you're in active contact with the present moment, and anxiety is a problem for you, your solution is to simply remain in constant contact with the present moment, right?

Well, as Burns suggested, that kind of complete present moment contact is just great for mice, but it's a real problem for us humans, who have a little quirk called language that tends to get in the way of living only in the moment.

Words can make monsters present. Not only *can* words evoke the past or conjure the future, dragging them unbidden into the present, they often do exactly that—sometimes for whole lifetimes. It's very easy to observe that the phenomenon of anxiety can't persist in the present moment, but this, too, is something of a language game. It's one thing to observe it, another thing entirely to make words into deeds and actually experience your life with a clear focus on the present. In other words, to stay connected to the present, you need to practice, practice, practice.

Learning to stay more closely connected to the present moment is a skill you can nurture for a lifetime. It amounts to a long journey. And even the longest journey begins with a single step (sorry for the cliché).

Mindfulness

Mindfulness is an ancient concept. It's often associated with Buddhism, in which, as *right mindfulness*, it figures as one element of the *noble eightfold path* that leads away from suffering and toward self-awakening. Still, mindfulness isn't necessarily a religious or esoteric practice. It's just one particular way you can choose to experience the world. This particular kind of practice has been known for millennia, by nearly all of the world's cultures, for the benefits it offers those who choose to take it up: clarity of vision, compassion, thoughtfulness, and peace of mind. Because of these benefits, expressions of mindfulness may be found in the contemplative traditions of many of the world's religions, including Christianity, Judaism, Islam, Hinduism, and others. But there's nothing religious, supernatural, or otherworldly in mindfulness at all. Quite the contrary, it's about being fully and intentionally connected to the very earthly here and now. And we are, for all of that, really just interested in the effect that being more connected to the present moment might have on your experience of anxiety.

More than anyone, noted author and researcher Jon Kabat-Zinn has promoted a secular understanding of the idea of mindfulness. His ideas have grown into a therapeutic model called *mindfulness-based stress reduction (MBSR)*, which has helped a lot of people make progress on issues of physical and emotional pain. We're deeply indebted to him for our interest in and understanding of mindfulness, and you'll find several of his works recommended in the section "Sources for Further Study."

Kabat-Zinn famously defined mindfulness as "the awareness that emerges through paying attention on purpose, in the present moment, and nonjudgmentally, to the unfolding of experience moment by moment" (Kabat-Zinn 1994, 4). To his very functional definition of the quality of mindfulness, we'll add a couple of fine points: Though the attention you bring to the unfolding of experience in the present moment should be deliberate and purposeful, it should also be relatively flexible. That is to say, you should be aware of the present moment but not entranced by it. If the walls fall down around you, you should notice that this is happening rather than be obliviously transfixed on some focus of your attention. Think back to the example of computer game play, during which time you might be very focused on what's happening on the screen in the present moment but be totally disconnected from the world around you. And while your goal in mindfulness should be to pay attention on purpose to the unfolding of experience moment to moment, you shouldn't try too hard to pay attention to *every* experience that might happen to unfold. This kind of distractibility shows a lot of flexibility, but it doesn't achieve the deliberateness and focus that characterizes mindful moments.

We'll call your attention to a fine point in Kabat-Zinn's definition, one that reveals a catch, a subtle and important catch, in mindfulness practice, especially mindfulness practice as you might encounter it in a volume like this one. That catch hinges on the word "emerges." There's a spontaneity and naturalness in that word, and this sense of things "just happening" matters a lot. There are a lot of books on the market that adapt mindfulness for this purpose or that. Please understand that this isn't one of them. While we're asserting that more complete and consistent contact with the present moment will quite naturally temper your experience of anxiety, we're also strongly of the opinion that any attempts you make at practicing mindfulness for the *purpose* of reducing anxiety are likely to meet with failure.

Why? Remember Kabat-Zinn's definition: mindfulness happens when you "pay...attention on purpose, in the present moment, and nonjudgmentally, to the unfolding of experience moment by moment." It's not really possible to pay careful, nonjudgmental atten-tion to the unfolding of experience when, all the while, you're evalu-ating whether or not your efforts so far have "worked." You might count your breaths or your footfalls, or listen to the crashing of waves on the beach, but if the *real* focus of your attention is whether or not your anxiety is diminishing—well, that looks a lot like even more anxiety. The purpose of mindfulness, at least from an ACT perspec-tive, is to bring you more intimately into contact with the richness of your life, not to reduce anxiety. From your first exercise through a lifetime of practice, your goal is the same: to simply observe what *is* as it happens. To that end, here's another game.

Game: Just a Minute
Props: A minute timer • **Difficulty:** Easy

Most of us feel, at least every so often, that time is getting away from us, that there just aren't enough hours in the day. But just how long is an hour, really?—or a minute? This game can help you get a sense of how connected you are to the actual passing of time. If you find that you often feel hurried, it may be that you sense time passing more quickly than it really does. On the other hand, if your perception of time runs too slowly, you may find that you're often late for things. Once you've played this game, you'll have a good idea whether your internal clock runs fast or slow. If you have a history of trouble with anxiety, here's a bet: we think your clock will run fast, speeding you through the game in anticipation of whatever comes next. Of course, that's not necessarily so, but the odds are definitely with us. At the end of the game, you'll also know what it feels like to be very attentive and focused for just one minute, which, repeated over and over again, is all a mindfulness practice really is.

1. Sit comfortably in a chair or on a cushion in a quiet part of your home or in some peaceful setting at a time when you're not likely to be disturbed.

2. Loosen anything you're wearing that might restrict your breathing, such as your collar or belt. Get comfortable. If you're wearing a watch, take it off, but keep it close at hand.

3. Take a few deep breaths. Once you do, take a look at your watch. As the sweep hand passes the twelve, set your watch aside or turn it over in your hand so that you can't see the face.

4. Now just sit comfortably and breathe normally until you sense that one minute has elapsed. (Oh, and don't

cheat by counting the seconds. It may be tempting, but it defeats the purpose of the game.)

5. Check your watch, and note how much time has passed.

How did it go? Do you feel as if you have a good sense of time, or were you surprised by how long or short your minute actually was? Remember that your purpose here is to develop an intentional and attentive relationship with the present moment, and becoming sensitive to the rate at which time passes is a good place to start. Think about what the results of this exercise might mean for you. Also, you may want to make a note of where your thoughts wandered while you were waiting for the minute to go by. After you've practiced the techniques for a while, you might want to play this game again to see if your perception of time has become more accurate.

The Rhythm of Attention

Let's go a little further into the idea that intentional, flexible contact with the present moment is in some way incompatible with feelings of anxiety. What is it about sitting quietly and paying attention to the present moment that can influence your experience of anxiety?

If you think back to our discussion of the function of anxiety in chapter 2, you'll recall that one of the principal reasons we get anxious is to protect ourselves from anticipated pain. In the case of fear—where we perceive a specific source of imminent harm, as distinct from anxiety—our defensive actions can be very fast and very focused. If a squirrel sees a fox bearing down on her with its teeth bared, she'll run as fast as she can toward a hole in the rock that's big enough for her to fit through but too small to admit the fox. If she stops to pay careful, focused attention to the experience as it unfolds in the present moment, she'll end up being the fox's lunch. Similarly, let's say you're walking along a busy street with a friend who's telling you a funny joke. She's about to get to the punch line when the two of you hear squealing tires and breaking glass. What do you do? Do you turn to your friend and ask, "So what *did* the farmer say to the traveling salesman?" Of course, you don't. You stop and turn all of your faculties to identifying which car has careered out of control and to seeing if you need to run or take cover. Like the fox-haunted squirrel, if you need to act to protect yourself, you're likely to do so without much thought, figuring out where it's safe to be and getting there fast.

And there's the rub: fast. When the squirrel sees the fox or you hear squealing tires, these perceptions are indications of real and present threats. But when you feel anxious and aren't quite sure what it is that's about to harm you, your tendency is still to act fast to protect yourself. You identify a thing, person, or situation that you feel uneasy about; you identify a place where you think you'll feel safe; and you get there—fast.

Think back to the game earlier in this chapter where we used the narrative example of Bernice in the lunchroom. You have your brown bag in hand, and you're making your way to the table. You notice Bernice eyeing you over her ham sandwich. Unlike in the game, don't imagine that she actually tells you what she thinks of you. Just let it be the case that she might do something, anything. You actually have no idea what might happen if you sit down at the table with Bernice and your other coworkers. How would you feel if she called you out, embarrassed you in front of your peers? What would it be like to be in that awkward, painful situation? What would you do to spare yourself that pain? You might think of yourself like a squirrel and your desk like a hole in the rocks. Bernice might, in that moment, become like a hungry fox, and you might need to hightail it out of there—fast.

Or you could slow down. Your situation is very different from the squirrel's. Bernice may be many things, but a vicious cannibal is probably not one of them. There's a slim chance that she might say some hurtful things to you, and if she did, it would likely be pretty unpleasant. But you'd still get to go home at five o'clock with all of your body parts intact.

If you were to approach the lunchroom slowly, paying careful attention to your experience of the moment, to the sensations that come up in your body with each step, you might notice your overwhelming urge to flee start to lose its hold over you. Here comes a knot in your stomach. There it goes. Now there's sweat rolling down your side. Okay, that's gone now. You're thinking that Bernice is sure to lunge at you at any moment. Now she's fiddling with the tab on her can of diet soda. You take your seat. The guy next to you greets you. Even Bernice nods in your direction. Or maybe she starts to rant at you. You just have to wait and see what happens.

Notice that at no point in the interaction does your anxiety go away. It's still there, because that's how you're inclined to react to situations where you perceive that things might go terribly, horribly wrong. But when you move at a slow and deliberate pace, sensations that you might have previously found intolerable will have a chance to fade over time. You might have a chance to realize that there are more options open to you than just running. You may find that you can live with the pounding in your chest and the butterflies in your stomach—if these things occur in the service of something that matters to you, like feeling collegial and connected to your coworkers during the lunch hour. But none of these realizations will be open to you unless you slow down and take the time to notice them. In other words, they will remain hidden to you as long as you keep living your life ten minutes into the future rather than firmly in the present moment.

This next game will help you learn to slow down. Breath counting is a lot of people's first experience of mindfulness. People start here, and they often go much deeper into their practice—or, more correctly, they often continue their practice for a long time, since breath-counting meditation is not only simple but also very profound.

Game: Inhale, Exhale, Repeat
Props: A cushion or comfortable chair, a timer of some kind • **Difficulty:** Easy at first, but harder the longer you sustain your practice

Mindful breathing is perhaps the practice most commonly associated with mindfulness—and with good reason. In order to train yourself to be fully aware of the present moment, it helps to have something to focus on. You could choose anything, really, but there are several advantages to choosing the breath. For one thing, it's free. And it's always conveniently available whenever you choose to pay attention to it. The breath also connects you to the physical world around you. And, when you really watch it closely, you'll discover that there are things about your breathing that you might never have even imagined: its depth, cadence, the small details of its movement through your nose and into your lungs, the way it feels inside your chest. In all, it's a terrific object for mindful study.

Your initial attempts at breath counting should be short. Three minutes is a good place to start, but even this is a long time to remain focused on your breath. If you find this too challenging, you can start with just a single minute. Progressively increase your practice periods until you can sit with your breath for at least fifteen, thirty, or even forty-five minutes. How long you can sit is less important, though, than sitting regularly. Many people find it helpful to set aside shorter practice periods in the morning and the evening. Remember that this is your practice; whatever's comfortable for you and gets you closer to your goal of paying attention to the present moment is the "right" approach for you.

We describe how to do this simple technique below, and we recommend that you use it when you first begin your practice. Breath counting will help you keep your focus when your mind starts to wander. But do look forward to a time when you can stop counting your breath and simply focus on each inhalation and exhalation as it happens.

As you watch your breathing, pay attention to all of the physical sensations that are part of the process: the rise and fall of your stomach and chest, that cool sensation on your upper lip and inside your nostrils, the feel of pressure in your lungs. As you practice, become aware of subtler details in your breathing, making this an ever-richer exercise.

1. To keep track of your practice, find some kind of timer. A kitchen timer, watch, or cell phone with an alarm will work, but all of these tend to go off like smoke alarms when their time is up. For a gentler conclusion to your practice, you might look online for simple software applications specifically for meditation timing. When they go off, they generally sound soft tones or even electronic versions of gongs or temple bells. These will be much less jarring than the scream of your alarm clock.

2. Pick a quiet place for your practice in your home or in some natural setting. Choose a location that will be more or less free from distracting noises, sights, and smells. You can sit on a cushion on the floor or in a chair, but try to find an arrangement that allows you to sit comfortably with your back straight. Lower your eyelids slightly and direct your gaze at a spot on the floor or ground a few feet in front of you. You can close your eyes if you like. If you find yourself getting drowsy or if you feel disoriented with your eyes closed, you can try keeping them open slightly, with your gaze soft and lowered to the floor in front of you.

3. Start your timer, and then take three very deep, very slow breaths. After you exhale the third deep breath, breathe normally, without making any special attempt to control or regulate the rate or depth of the breaths you take in.

4. Let your breath fall down into your belly. When your belly is full, let your breath continue to rise into your chest. When you exhale, reverse the process.

5. When you are comfortable with the rhythm of your breath, you can begin the breath-counting exercise. On an inhalation, count "one." Then let your breath exhale naturally. On your next inhalation, count "two." Repeat this process until you come to "ten," counting only when you inhale. Don't worry if you lose count or repeat a number. Just pick a place to begin again.

6. After you complete a cycle of ten breaths, spend a little while paying attention to any physical sensations you may feel. Notice the mechanics of your breathing, the sensation of the cushion or chair beneath you, the feel of the air against your skin. Listen for any subtle sounds that would otherwise escape you. Pay attention to even the slightest details, like the feel of your clothing against your skin or the weight of your hair against your collar or shoulders.

7. After a period of body awareness, repeat the breath-counting exercise for another cycle of ten breaths.

8. All the while, you'll notice that thoughts pop into your head. When this happens, acknowledge them and let them go. Gently return your attention back to your breathing. You may find that you can focus more effectively when counting breaths or when focusing on physical sensations. Slip into whichever practice works best for you when thoughts arise.

9. Wandering thoughts are not a problem. They are entirely usual, to be expected and welcomed as part of the process. Observing a return to the breath is as important and valuable as attending to it constantly.

10. When your timer goes off, take three more deep, slow breaths. Then allow your eyes to open fully, and return your awareness to the room. You may want to take a few moments to gently stretch or take a short walk if your legs or back have become a little tight and fatigued from sitting.

Learning from Your Demons

At this point, we should probably warn you against being dogmatic about remaining in contact with the present moment. Remember, above all, flexibility of behavior is our goal—your goal, if you want to be able to live your life in a way that matters to you even as you experience feelings of anxiety. Living in closer contact with your reality of the moment is one way to mitigate the effects of anxiety on your life, but it isn't the only way. Be cautious about setting down one burden only to pick up another.

Mindful attention to the present moment is a good thing, but it's not the only thing. Daydreaming involves a loss of contact with the events around us. On a spring day while lying out on a blanket in the warm sun, daydreaming can be a fine thing to do. We recommend it. But the same act of daydreaming while driving can be disastrous. The trick is to learn to tell the difference between when it's important to remain in the present and when it isn't, and to have the ability to bring your attention to bear when it serves your values.

How do you develop the ability to discriminate? All of us learn from, and are shaped by, our interactions with the environment, and in order to receive the environment's instruction, we need to be there to interact with it. This doesn't merely mean that you must be there physically. You need to be psychologically present. If you have a fear of dogs or spiders, for example, you must interact with dogs or spiders in a variety of ways in order for their fearsomeness to recede. Sitting in the classroom daydreaming and looking at the clouds won't help you learn algebra. To learn algebra, you must interact with formulas, numbers, variables, and so forth. To interact effectively with the complex world around you—your work, family, friendships, and so forth—you have to be open to what the situations you encounter have to teach you. These situations can't and won't teach you what works unless you find inside yourself the capacity to listen to them, to pay attention to them purposefully in the moment.

You probably see where we're heading with this. The things you feel anxious about can actually teach you a lot about how you can and should operate in the world. Insight isn't the only thing, but it is something. If you continually have painful experiences in a particular area of your life, what do those experiences have to teach you about how the world works? About how you can best function in it? Going to these places can be scary, we realize. But, again, going slow can make the difference between exploring hard places and running from them. With that in mind, here's our last game of the chapter. It offers you a way to play around with seeing what your anxiety can teach you about the world.

Game: Feeding Anxiety
Props: None, just your imagination •
Difficulty: Hard

This game is somewhat involved, so you should probably have some practice under your belt before trying it. It's not that it's all that complicated; like the other games in this chapter, it just invites things that are already present to come more clearly into focus. But it does involve a fair amount of visualization, and it has a number of steps that you'll want to have committed to memory before you start—and this can be a bit much to handle if you're not used to these kinds of experiences. If you have trouble keeping all of the steps in your mind when you try the game, you might want to record the steps on a handheld recorder or your computer, making your own guided audio meditation. This can be fun, and it can make this particular exercise doubly powerful.

Basically, this exercise is about taking a thought that's disturbing to you and getting to know it better. This might be a little unnerving at first. If you feel that this exercise is too much for you to do alone, just leave it be. You can either come back to it another day or simply do other mindfulness exercises that you are more comfortable with. But part of the goal of this work is for you to learn to recognize your anxious thoughts as what they are: thoughts, events that you can acknowledge and let pass. By imagining that your anxious thought has physical qualities, you can learn to look at it in a new way and maybe even learn to appreciate it as a part of you that needs to be treated with kindness and compassion.

1. Find someplace comfortable before you begin this game—sitting in a firm chair, on a cushion, or out in the sunshine. Inhale and exhale three times, deeply and slowly. Then spend a few minutes concentrating on your breath. You can go through a few cycles of breath counting, if you want to.

2. Once you're settled into your breathing, allow your mind to focus on some anxious thought that has been troubling you.

3. Watch this thought. Allow it to take on a shape in your mind. It could be egg shaped, hard edged like a cube, or jumbled up like a raked-together pile of leaves. Whatever shape it takes is all right. When your thought has a definite shape, allow it to take on a color. Maybe it will be bright red or pale gray, green like a watermelon or brown like a tree trunk. Let your awareness settle on the color and shape of your distressing thought. Finally, let your thought take on the form of some kind of being. Allow it to have features that you can recognize: a face with eyes, a nose, ears, and a mouth. Your thought may have arms and legs, wings, or a tail. It may seem friendly or threatening,

but just watch it. Know that it's just a thought and that it can't harm you.

4. Now that your thought has a form, imagine where it is in your body. Is it floating inside your head or is it moving around in your chest? Maybe it's at your finger-tips or underneath your backside as you sit there. It may be motionless, or it could be moving around inside you. Whatever it's doing, become aware of it inside you.

5. Now invite your thought outside of your body. Don't do this in the spirit of casting it away. Just bring it outside of yourself so that you can take it in with perspective, so that you can see it from a different angle and in a differ-ent light. Your thought might sit across the room from you or float over your head. Notice your thought, and just let it do what it needs to do.

6. Once you've become fully aware of your thought outside your body, ask it the question, "What do you need?" Then just listen to the answer it gives you. When it answers you, think for a moment about what it says. Try to sense whether it has told you what it really needs or if it has just told you what it wants. If you need to, ask it again what it needs. Your thought might tell you that it needs to be certain, that it needs to be safe, or that it needs to be loved and protected. Whatever your thought has to say, just watch and listen.

7. Sit quietly with the thought for a few moments. Next, imagine that you could offer a small gift to that thought— some small kindness.

8. When you have fed your thought, invite it back inside of yourself. Remember that your thought is something that you have. Your goal is not to push it away or get rid of it. Instead, you want to learn how to have it gently and

without judgment, allowing it to come and go without effort.

9. Once your thought is back inside yourself, return your focus to your breath. Count through a cycle of ten normal breaths, followed by three deep, slow breaths. Then gently open your eyes and allow your attention to come back to the room.

This game sometimes takes people by surprise. If you've spent a lot of time struggling with anxious thoughts, it can seem very strange to not only spend some time with them on purpose but also to feed and take care of them. But there's a certain paradoxical wisdom to this kind of visualization. By befriending your anxious thoughts, you may be less likely to be vexed by them in the future. Instead of threatening, scary manifestations, they may start to seem to you like scared kids that need a helping hand. As you treat them with kindness and compassion, you'll be more likely to extend the same care and concern to yourself. Over time, you may find that you're less critical and more accepting of yourself at times when your anxiety runs high. (Oh, and this idea will be a big deal in the chapter on self-as-context, just so you know.)

With practice, you'll find that you can start to find the space to move, even when you're in the presence of anxiety. You'll start to feel as if you might be able to actively make room for your anxious thoughts. And this brings us to our next process discussion: defusion.

4

Tell

Me a

Story:

Defusion

Perception of an

Object costs

Precise the Object's loss.

Perception in itself a gain

Replying to its price;

The Object Absolute is nought,

Perception sets it fair,

And then upbraids a Perfectness

That situates so far.

—Emily Dickinson, "Perception"

There's an old campfire story about a nervous man who's afraid of the dark, living by himself in a rundown house. Every night he lies awake, terrified by every bump and creak he hears. Finally, in a desperate attempt to calm his nerves, he buys a pistol. At first, the weapon seems to do him some good. He still doesn't sleep soundly much of the time, but when he's the most scared, he reaches under his pillow, pulls out the pistol, and aims it at the door. After a while, when nothing comes bursting in upon him, he feels a little better. He slips the gun back under the pillow and eventually falls asleep.

This arrangement works out for a time. But one sultry night, the man wakes up from an uneasy dream. Everything is silent—maybe too silent. The light of a full moon is streaming through the window as he looks around the room. He's about to put his head back on the pillow when he looks to the foot of the bed, where, to his great horror, he sees two eyes shining evilly up at him. His heart races, and he doesn't dare to breathe. Slowly, slowly he reaches for the pistol. He points the barrel of the gun right between the eyes and wraps his finger around the trigger. After a moment, he finds his voice.

"Get out!" he cries. "Or I'll shoot!"

The thing at the end of the bed just stares back at him, icy and unblinking.

"I mean it!" he shrieks again. He bolts upright in bed, whereupon the thing starts to lunge toward him. He fires one shot.

And then he shrieks again, for he has just shot his big toe clean off—which, like its counterpart on the other foot, has been sticking out of the covers, the nail reflecting the moonlight like the eye of some ravening monster.

Going Down with a Thinking Ship

It's a silly old story, mostly good for scaring the kids at Halloween. But its premise is relevant to our discussion in this chapter—and it's not because the hero of the story is apparently an anxiety sufferer. His story interests us most when we consider the mental quirk that led him to shoot off his toe.

The man in the story maims his foot because he thinks his big toes are actually the eyes of some monster that has come to eat him up in the night. And by shooting at the monster, he hopes to drive it away, kill it, or otherwise prevent it from doing him harm. It's a simple-enough formulation: Monsters are bad. If one shows up, do what you can to get away from it or, barring that, make it go away.

His thinking doesn't stand up to much scrutiny, though, if we puzzle it through from the comfort and security of our couches (or wherever it is you're sitting and reading). Is our hero familiar with how monster eyes look in the dark? Is he, in fact, accustomed to finding monsters lurking at the foot of his bed—or even accustomed to encountering them at all? If his experience is anything like that of the rest of us, the answer is no. And even if you take the leap and grant the existence of monsters, would shooting in the direction of your own feet be the best course of action even if there happened to be one down thataway?

Reason it however you like, but the story stays the same: Our hero sees two round, shiny things at the end of the bed, thinks they're the eyes of a monster, and—bang! He acts accordingly.

We can abstract this situation into a formulation:

I thought X, so I did Y.

Where X = (some scary thought)

Where Y = (some act that has consequences for our lives or the lives of others)

This formulation isn't limited to campfire stories. If you doubt this, just point a Web browser to your favorite news search engine, and type in "shot mistaken identity." You'll find that the formulation "I thought he was someone else, so I shot him" is tragically common.

You can take your investigations further, if you like. Go to your local library or jump on the Internet and see if you can find an example of the formulation, "I think bad blood is the cause of certain diseases, so I'll treat your sore throat, fever, and chills by making deep incisions in your forearms, which I will allow to bleed freely for some time." Here's a hint to get you started: find a biography of George Washington and flip to the end.

These examples are theatrical and flamboyant, but this formulation isn't limited to nighttime misadventure and eighteenth-century quackery. Consider these examples:

- I think I'm unlikable and I bore people, so I'll skip that party I really want to go to.

- I think I'm irresponsible and immature, so I could never be a good parent.

- I'm lazy and really pretty stupid, so I won't take on that challenging project at work or speak up in the next staff meeting.

Hmmm. It does appear that there's a connection between what we think and how we feel and act. And some of our thoughts do seem directly relevant to the things we feel anxious about in life. Maybe we're really onto something now.

Treading Water in the Tide of Your Thoughts

Let's not be hasty, though. It's tempting to interpret the previous section to mean that our feelings of anxiety are the result of inaccurate thinking—with believing that there are monsters at the foot of the bed and whatnot. And we might take this realization as a prescription to figure out which of our thoughts are accurate and which aren't, and then set about to change them.

And if we did think this way, we'd be in very good company: we'd be coming to some of the same conclusions as many of the best minds in psychology during the latter half of the twentieth century. These decades were marked by the rise of the various cognitive therapies, approaches to psychotherapy that looked to distorted or irrational thinking as the possible cause for problems such as anxiety, depression, and so forth. These approaches were very significant advances to psychotherapy at the time. They extended therapists' repertoires well beyond the Freudian directive to look for the causes of mental disturbance in unconscious emotions and drives, and they developed a strong base of scientific evidence to support the conclusion that psychotherapy really *did* something to improve the mental health of the people who received it.

It's very easy to see the connection between our thoughts and our moods, emotions, and so forth. It turns out, though, that it's not so easy to monitor, manipulate, or modify those thoughts in order to change how we feel.

If we consider the examples of the monster-eye guy and the Revolutionary-era surgeon, it's pretty easy for us to conclude that the problem lies with the "X" in our formulation—with the inaccurate thoughts that lead to the regrettable actions. If you think something cockamamie—that your toe is a monster's eye or that bad blood causes the common cold—you're apt to do reckless and dangerous things like shooting yourself in the foot or bleeding your already weakened and dehydrated patients to death. And this extends easily to the more mundane examples we offered of thoughts you might have about yourself: If you think you're unlikable and boring—despite the fact that any number of people find you lovable and fascinating—you're likely to hide yourself away and avoid parties. The firmly held conviction that you're a feckless adolescent, irrespective of the fact that you pay your bills on time and have a nurturing streak a mile wide, will dissuade you from making the choice to start a family—and so forth.

The erroneous contents of your thoughts *seem* to be the source of the problems. So "change 'X' and you'll change 'Y'" looks like a pretty good plan. Change the content of your error-ridden or distorted thinking, and you'll change the way you feel and, thereafter, the way you interact with the world. At least it *sounds* great.

But here's an example to consider: Imagine a man who has a history of suffering from episodes of panic. From time to time, while he's in the middle of what appears to be a normal, nonthreatening situation, he's overwhelmed with the idea that he's in some kind of danger that he can't easily escape. He feels weak and nauseated; he starts to hyperventilate; and he feels intense, stabbing pain in his chest. He thinks, in short, that he's having a heart attack, which leads him to panic more, which in turn makes the symptoms worse. Now further imagine that this guy actually *is* at very high risk for a heart attack. Four of his coronary arteries are 80 percent blocked, and what he feels in his chest *is* actually angina. In this case, his thoughts contain content that's actually accurate, although they still work in the same way as inaccurate ones to throw gasoline on the fire of his anxiety.

And here's another example. Imagine a college student struggling academically who reports that she feels shy and awkward in social situations. She describes feeling reluctant to participate in her classes or engage socially with other students. She feels overwhelmed by the material being taught in her courses, and she thinks she'll appear stupid if she asks questions and tries to participate in class. Furthermore, she thinks she's unlikable and imagines she'll be rejected by others if she tries to engage them in conversation during her off hours. It would be good natured of us to conclude that this young woman is poised and intelligent, that she's merely the victim of her inaccurate and punishing critical inner voice. But the simple truth is that some of the stuff they teach in college is hard. It's probably true that our friend *will* make some mistakes when she begins to participate in her classes, and it's possible that some of the quicker students might make fun of her—it has been known to happen. And risk taking in social situations is well known to be fraught with peril. In a nutshell, the thoughts that our young friend is having are quite possibly accurate. We all can point to at least anecdotal evidence to support the conclusion that she'll actually experience the painful situations she worries about. But if she wants to become accomplished in her studies or better able to enjoy socializing, she needs to participate in class and engage with others, whatever it is that she might be thinking. What will happen if, through some means or the other, our friend manages to change her thinking? What's likely to happen if she disputes and silences the thought, "If I speak up in class, I'll make a fool of myself and people will laugh at me," and then, in the middle of her American History section, she blurts out that George Washington signed the Emancipation Proclamation on the beach in Santa Monica? Yep. She's in for a pretty hard fall.

Maybe the content of our thoughts isn't the end of the story after all. And even if we suspend our judgment about that issue for a while, there's another, bigger problem. Evaluating a thought for accuracy and actually changing it are two *very* different things. All of us are prone to making big deals out of ideas that, in the end, turn out to be pretty minor. If you struggle with anxiety, this scenario isn't foreign to you. The presentation you dread for months comes and goes without so much as a hiccup; the plane brings you home safely from your tropical vacation, and the worst part of the flight was the food. Yes, you can tell yourself that there's nothing to worry about. We suspect you've done a fair bit of that in your life. But maybe that telling led you to spend hours trying very hard to figure out whether or not there was really something worth worrying about. And, well, there you were, worrying again. If you've spent any time and effort trying to change, stop, or mitigate your thoughts, how has that worked for you? If you're like a lot of people, it probably hasn't worked very well.

Let's put this whole thought-changing business to the test. But let's not try it with something hard, like a thought you connect to feelings of anxiety. Let's play a game with a thought that's more or less totally inconsequential and totally random.

Game: Not Thinking About a Guy Named Lester
Props: Some kind of timer for round 1; a scrap of paper, a pen, and a short piece of string for round 2 • **Difficulty:** Impossible

According to the Baby Name Wizard website (www. babynamewizard.com), which collects and analyzes name data from the Social Security Administration, the name Lester peaked in popularity in the 1910s, at which time about fifteen hundred babies in every million were given the name. After World War I, the popularity of the name dropped steadily for some reason. Today, fewer than a hundred babies per million are pinned with the moniker. We think it's pretty likely that you don't know anyone with that name. But if you do, terrific. This game will be even more fun for you.

If you *don't* know anyone named Lester, read the following paragraph several times, slowly and carefully:

Lester is a thirty-eight-year-old man. Lester is tall, with short brown hair and a slightly receding hairline. Lester has brown eyes and high cheekbones. Lester is clean shaven and dresses professionally. Lester has a prominent scar on his right cheek, the result of a skiing accident he had when he was a boy. Lester lives in Albuquerque, New Mexico.

If you *do* know someone named Lester, take two or three minutes to sit quietly and reflect on everything you know about the man in your life: how he looks, how he spends his time, how he interacts with you, and so forth.

Once you've finished one or the other of the above tasks, get ready to play the game.

Round 1: Set your timer for two minutes. If any significant time has passed since you read the paragraph above or reflected on your own personal Lester, repeat that step. Now, start your timer. Your goal in round 1 is to *not* think about Lester. You may think of anything *except* Lester. And remember, thinking such thoughts as "I must not think about Lester" is really thinking about Lester, so don't try to be funny!

Round 2: After you've finished round 1, take your string and tie it around your index finger. On the scrap of paper, write the word "Lester" with the pen. Fold the paper and place it in your pocket. Now go about the rest of your day. As you're doing whatever it is that you do, you'll notice from time to time that you have a string on your finger. When you notice it, don't think about Lester and don't think about the piece of paper in your pocket.

Well, what do you think? Did you discover by playing this game, that your mind is like the serve-yourself soda fountain at your local fast-food restaurant? That you can turn it on and off as you like, and you can freely choose what flows out of it?

No? Well, we kind of knew that. Winning round 1 of the game is impossible, even if you've never met anyone named Lester in your whole life. Round 2, with reminders *to* think of Lester is, well, even more impossible. And what do you think it would be like if we could somehow direct you to play a third round of the game, a round that you prepare for by thinking about and being reminded about Lester every few days or hours for your *entire life*?

Think back to the examples of thought formulations we gave you earlier, even the silly ones. How many times do you suppose the man in the story had had the thought "Monsters are waiting to get me"? And if any of the other three examples struck you as familiar, how many times have you rehearsed the thought "I'm unlikable," "I'm irresponsible," or "I'm lazy"?

We're not disputing the idea that the contents of our thoughts influence the way we act. But changing the contents of our thoughts in order to change the way we act? That's tough, as the game we just played demonstrates pretty clearly. Thoughts are made of words, and your mind is a finely tuned word-generating machine, whether you want it to be or not.

Nevertheless, this control-your-thoughts strategy is rather widely accepted, both by the psychological profession and by popular culture. The story of how this strategy evolved in the psychological community is a long one—and it's probably more interesting to a few of us than it would be to the rest. Suffice it to say that, through the latter half of the twentieth century and up to the present, many psychologists have had confidence in this strategy, and they've taught it to their clients without reservation. At the same time, the popular media has reinforced the strategy: positive thinking and a positive self-esteem, both the expression of the contents of thinking, are widely held to be good things. Yet at least one recent study has even shown that positive self-statements, such as "I am a lovable person," may actually make individuals with low self-esteem feel *worse* (Wood, Perunovic, and Lee 2009).

Confused yet? That's no surprise. Like the rest of us, you've grown up in a culture that places a lot of value on the contents of thoughts— and one that has focused a lot of attention on the ways we can change those contents from bad to good. But let's go back to the abstraction of our thought formulation and take another look.

I thought X, so I did Y.

Where X = (scary thought)

Where Y = (some act that has consequences for our lives or the lives of others)

What if we could change that formulation just a little? What if we could make it work a little more to our advantage *without* going to the trouble of trying to change the content of "X," which we've seen is a very tall order? How about something like this?

I thought X. I did Y.

Where X = (anything at all that the mind can cook up, which we hold lightly)

Where Y = (some act that we have chosen, deliberately and mindfully, that moves us closer to something we value)

This formulation looks like the first one, but if you climb inside and try it out, you'll find that it feels *very* different. Lots of possibilities that might have been overshadowed by "X" start to reemerge once you start investing them with a little less power. In ACT-speak, this formulation is called *defusion*.

Rising to the Challenge of Not Believing Everything You Think

The word "defusion" is totally made up. You won't find it in a dictionary. The word reflects the notion that you can literally "fuse" with a thought, the way two pieces of hot plastic might fuse together to become one object. Defusion describes a state in which we regard the contents of our thoughts as just what they are: a collection of words that form in our minds. Depending on how useful they are in our lives, we may act upon them, or we may not. But we get to choose.

There's an opposite state to defusion, which, because psychologists are a creative bunch, is known as *fusion*. Fusion describes a state in which we take our thoughts literally, investing them with consequence and authority. Fusion comes with a sense of urgency—a sense that something *must* be done. When you're fused with a thought, your opportunities for action in areas related to that thought are always diminished. Fusion with the thought that you are boring and unlikable diminishes your opportunities in the area of socializing because, well, people *must* have better things to do than pal around with dull boors. Fusion with the thought that you are lazy and stupid limits what's possible for you at work—and so forth. It may sound totally strange, but from an ACT perspective, we're not especially concerned with the contents of thoughts and whether those contents are accurate. Instead, we want to know how *workable* those thoughts are in your life. We won't do much at all to test the accuracy of or to change your thoughts, but we'll work damn hard to get them to be more workable in the context of your life. We're chiefly interested in whether there's enough space between your thoughts and you to permit you to live in a rich and purposeful way.

Defusion isn't the same thing as debunking your thoughts or figuring out where you've made mistakes in thinking. In fact, merely knowing that you've had an erroneous thought won't do you much good at all. It's entirely common for people who worry about their health to "know" that they actually have clean bills of health and for people who are ill at ease in gatherings to "know" that others tend to find them charming. Defusion isn't the process of arguing with or disputing your thoughts at all. Rather, it's the process of holding *all* of your thoughts lightly enough to be able to do what you need to do in your life.

And we do mean *all* of your thoughts, even the ones that happen to be true. Consider again the student in a college class who thinks, "I'm the only one in the room who doesn't get this stuff, so I'll just keep my mouth shut and avoid looking like an idiot." What if this student really *was* the only one in the room struggling with the material? Would the truth of that thought justify her decision to sit quietly? Not if her intended goal was to learn the material being taught. She's faced with a rather painful choice: to speak up and reveal her ignorance or stay silent and remain ignorant. As we've seen before, both paths come with a fair amount of discomfort, but only one gets the student closer to where she wants to be in life.

How to Defuse

As we said, all by itself, knowing isn't especially valuable. So far in this chapter, we've made a case for not taking your thoughts too seriously, and maybe we've persuaded you to give it a try. So how do you do it?

The answer to that question begins with one of the really cool things about the ACT model. Remember how we said that each of the processes is reflected in the others? That's true, and there's a very intimate relationship between defusion and contact with the present moment. If you're tearing through life as fast as you can go, with your sights set on something, anything, out in the future, it's very likely that your thoughts of the moment will exercise a lot of control over your actions. Slowing down, even a little, is a good way to start seeing when you're acting automatically on some thought you've had. And the games in the last chapter are all good ways to learn how to slow down.

Has your car ever made a disconcerting noise while you were driving, only to run silent and tight as a drum when you took it to the mechanic? It's hard for the mechanic to fix a noise that she can't hear—but she's a busy woman, with lots of cars to see to in a day. If she had the time to sit quietly with your car as it rolled down the road, she would eventually hear the sound and have some idea of how to make it stop. It's kind of like that with your thoughts—only the hourly rate you pay to sit and pay attention to your thoughts is much lower than what your mechanic charges. The game "Inhale, Exhale, Repeat" from the last chapter is a good way to get started. You can play that game anytime you suspect you're struggling with a fused thought. If it's not obvious to you what the problem is, sit with it for a while. It'll show up eventually. When it does, you'll be ready. You can think of this as catching the thought "in flight."

The last game in that chapter, "Feeding Anxiety," is another approach to dealing with fusion. Change the rules a little bit, replacing "something you feel anxious about" with "some thought you find yourself fusing with." Maybe it's "I'm lazy" or "I'll never be good enough" or "people don't like me." In the course of this game, as you invite the thought out of your body, give it qualities like shape, color, and texture; you'll change your relationship to it and reduce the degree of control it can assert over you without making any attempt to change its contents.

Here are a couple more games that can help you get a feel for defusion.

Game: You but Not You
Props: None • **Difficulty:** Easy

"If you want a job done right, do it yourself." Americans are a take-the-bull-by-the-horns kind of people. We descended from immigrants, pioneers, and homesteaders who toiled to make a life for ourselves and our children out of the wilderness—or at least that's how the story goes. Our culture values independence and self-reliance. And you folks in Canada, the UK, OZ, and New Zealand are equally as independent. Is it any wonder that we're liable to fuse with our thoughts? I mean, after all, they come from the source we tend to trust the most—ourselves.

But what if some of the stuff we think came from somewhere outside of our heads? You can fuse with the thought, "I'm pretty stupid, really," but what would happen if someone walked up to you and said that to your face? Odds are you would stare at him dumbfounded, run off in tears, or knock his teeth down his throat. But because the thought comes from you, well, it must really *mean* something. Ha!

In this game, you're going to try to imagine a thought you feel fused with coming from somebody or something *other* than you. Who or what that might be is limited only by your creativity and sense of humor. You get bonus points for coming up with something really good.

Start by getting comfortable in a place where you can play the game for a good five or ten minutes without being interrupted. Let the thought gather in your mind. Rehearse it a few times. Then conjure up the image of whoever or what-ever it is you're going to let articulate your thought.

If, for example, you find yourself getting caught on the thought, "I'm not a good-enough parent," you might imagine a full-grown pig sitting across the room from you, squeal-ing the thought in your direction. Maybe General George S. Patton, dressed in jackboots and a combat helmet, is barking the thought at you while standing in front of a huge American flag.

Whatever it is, keep in mind that the idea isn't to ridicule or make fun of *what* the thought has to say. Rather, the objec-tive is to hear the thought you find yourself getting stuck on in a voice other than your own, from somewhere other than inside your head. Set aside for a minute the obvious fact that the talking pig or the guy who looks a lot like George C. Scott really *is* inside your head. Just the shift from spontane-ously thinking the thought to conjuring it consciously and in an unusual context can help increase your sensitivity to those times when the thought is less than workable and is taking control of your life.

That game is a good one if you happen to be inclined to rumination. We've talked a lot about the content of thoughts, but we haven't spent any time on unbidden thoughts, reoc-curring notions that just spring to mind. They can really drive you crazy. After a conflict at work, for example, you might spend the afternoon (or the weekend or the whole next week) thinking, "Damn that guy! He must really hold me in contempt! Who does he think he is, anyway?!" This kind of thing can really be a drag for you to deal with, especially as the thoughts occur to you, coming into your awareness in your own voice. But what if a Cavalier King Charles spaniel were mouthing them? A toad? Even if the contents of the thought were the same, the source would change your rela-tionship to the thoughts themselves—and this might allow you to react to them differently.

Game: Broken Record
Props: None • **Difficulty:** Easy

What appears on the next two lines of this page?

CAT FERRET HAMSTER BUDGIE
GOLDFISH POT-BELLIED PIG

Answer out loud, right now, before you read on.

What did you just say? House pets? Animals? English words? A string of capital roman letters and spaces? Ink, pressed onto a sheet of paper in lines and curves? Or maybe a collection of dots on an electronic screen? If you think about it, any and all of these are true, but they surely don't all have the same implications, the same meaning.

The following is an old ACT game, one of the best known by people who are familiar with the work. It involves taking a word or idea and repeating it over and over again, until the spoken words dissolve into unintelligible sounds—simple music.

The game is at its most dramatic when the word or idea you choose is something you find very distressing. If you're very anxious about looking like a fool while giving a speech, you can say, "fool, fool, fool, fool, fool…" over and over. Keep going for at least a full minute. Eventually, your tongue will lose its ability to distinguish between the "ef" and the "el," and you'll sound like a barking sheepdog. After you're finished, sit for a minute with the idea of feeling like a fool, and see whether you don't feel a little freer.

From One Extreme to the Other: Fusing with Defusion

We mentioned in the last chapter that there's nothing inherently good about being in contact with the present moment. Likewise, there's nothing inherently good about defusion or bad about fusion. Neither is bad or good. Defusion and fusion simply are. In fact, there's an extraordinarily adaptive advantage to fusion. When one early caveman said to the other, "Don't go to the water hole; there's a lion there," if the other caveman responded to the word "lion" as if responding to an actual lion, he survived. Only one of these individuals actually saw the lion, the words of the other made the lion present for his friend. In the end, they both lived.

It's relatively simple to generate examples of fusion that are benign and sometimes even very helpful. For example, being deeply engaged with the words of a novel to the point where you lose awareness of things going on around you, and actually start to feel the suffering and joy of the characters, is good entertainment. If you're about to step into a crosswalk and someone shouts, "Watch out for that car!" you might leap from the street in response to the words in the same way that you might respond to the actual car. Here, the act of taking thoughts literally isn't just a nonproblem, it can also actually be a good thing.

Remember, though, that our goal is flexibility—the ability to do whatever we choose to do that gets us to where we want to go in life. When fusion gets in the way of the life you want to lead, it becomes a problem. Being enraptured by a novel on a Sunday afternoon is lovely; quitting your job and going on a three-week bender because your favorite character in a soap opera is killed off is something to be concerned about. Leaping to the curb when someone yells "Car!" is a good thing; sitting alone in your house every night because a voice in your head keeps shouting "Loser!" is a problem. It's part of the human condition that we create stories about ourselves and about the world around us. Our stories are often filled with limitations, and we proceed to live our lives inside those limitations. Your defusion work will help you do many things in the presence of a thought or a series of thoughts rather than only one thing. In other words, you'll be freer.

Notice that we didn't say your distressing thoughts will go away. They probably won't, and this brings us to our next process discussion: acceptance.

5

Come

What

May:

Acceptance

"Yes…" that peculiar
affirmative. "Yes…"
A sharp, indrawn breath,
half groan, half acceptance,
that means "Life's like that.
We know it (also death)."

—Elizabeth Bishop, "The Moose"

Let's recap a little: We're taking a look at the phenomenon of anxiety, the lingering, disconcerting sense that things might go terribly, horribly wrong. We've argued that anxiety is the by-product of some basic human tendencies, namely, our unease with ambiguity, and our tendency to solve problems where we find them and to create problems to solve where we don't. We've contended that the experience of anxiety is really not so different from the other kinds of problems with living that we all face, even though we've given it a name and some fancy, professional-sounding definitions. Suffering, we've suggested, is pretty much suffering. It's an experience common to us all, and it's an experience that we think has common roots in some basic problems in living. We've sought to describe these problems in living by looking at six areas of experience—and we've tried to examine the areas in terms that are relevant to the experience of anxiety.

So far, we've covered two of the six areas. Flexible and focused contact with the present moment, we've said, isn't compatible with anxiety, which arises only when we focus on a scary future or a corrupting past. We also took a look at the ways we sometimes take our thoughts literally and allow them to steer us in directions we don't want to go. The alternative to this literal fusion with the output of our minds is defusion, a state in which we hold lightly our thoughts about what we can and can't do.

Now, by way of introducing our third area for discussion, let's take a look at two short quotes.

Let me tell you the truth. The truth is, what is.
And what should be is a fantasy, a terrible
terrible lie that someone gave to the people long ago.

—Lenny Bruce, *How to Talk Dirty and Influence People*

And ye shall know the truth,
and the truth shall make you free.

—John 8:32

Weird juxtaposition, huh? The iconoclastic 1960s comedian who fought epic legal battles for the right to speak his mind to his audiences gives us a concise definition of the truth. "Look around you" is his implication. What you see with your eyes and hear with your ears is what you have to work with. Bruce goes on to characterize the notion that things "should" be some certain way, other than they are, in the worst terms. (It's interesting that Lenny Bruce shares his dislike of shoulds with one of the giants of cognitive behavioral therapy, the late Albert Ellis, who was well known for railing against both "should-ing" and "musterbation.") In the second quote, Jesus, as recorded in the Gospel of John, identifies truth as the agent of freedom. Reading the second quote in the light of the first gives us a neat synopsis of what we're going to look at in this chapter: our willingness to accept what's in our lives is an important part of breaking free from our problems in living, including anxiety.

Acceptance from an ACT Perspective

One of the ideas we've come back to a couple of times in this book is that there isn't anything necessarily bad about feeling anxious. It's all right to worry, fret, and panic. These are natural reactions that we all have in certain situations and, if you think back to our story about the bear and the blueberries, you might even agree that, sometimes, it's good to worry a little. It can help keep you from becoming somebody's lunch. Problems arise, though, when worrying, fretting, and panicking get between us and the things that matter to us in life. When you discover that your life is going unlived while you sit around beset with anxiety, that's a good time to start thinking about doing something different.

In the last chapter, we talked about how gripping onto our thoughts too tightly and letting them dictate our course in life can be a problem. In this chapter, we'll take a look at the closely related problem that occurs when we aren't willing to have the experiences that occur as we live our lives. This is one of the times when the ACT-speak for a problem comes pretty close to everyday speech. When we have this problem, we avoid certain experiences, so we call the problem *experiential avoidance*. We let go of this problem when we become willing to accept these same experiences, so—surprise, surprise—we call the process *acceptance*.

When we talk about acceptance in ACT, we mean adopting, on purpose, an open and receptive attitude toward the experiences we have as we live our lives, even when these experiences are strong negative judgments. The word "experience" here is used in a strict way to mean our private experience of the world: our thoughts and feelings, bodily sensations we may have, images and memories that might occur to us in certain situations. We're not speaking broadly about external events that happen in the world, like getting hit in the head by a stray golf ball or being chased down the street by a dog.

It's worth repeating that the kinds of private experiences we're talking about aren't limited to the kinds of thoughts we can put into words easily. Thoughts like "I'm going to make a fool of myself" and "He'll brush me off if I try to speak to him" are certainly part of the story. But so are urges, feelings, and sensations.

If you've ever tried to quit smoking, you'll be very familiar with these kinds of sensations: the automatic reach to the shirt pocket or purse for your pack, the pull you feel to light up in the morning with your coffee or after dinner. If you've never smoked, maybe you love sweets. You might then feel some of these sensations as you gaze at a cherry pie and wonder whether you'll have just one more slice. Call it longing, craving, or what you will, these experiences come up for all of us from time to time.

Following up on the example above, let's say you make the decision one afternoon to quit smoking for whatever reasons—it doesn't really matter what they are. The following morning, as you sit in the kitchen with your coffee *not* smoking, you have a particular set of experiences. Maybe you have the thought, "I'm going to go nuts if I don't have a cigarette." You feel a tightness in your chest. Your head hurts and your hands shake a little. You start to imagine what it felt like to take that first drag in the morning, something you did only yesterday. Maybe you think about what mornings from now on will be like without your trusty pack close at hand. Chances are you'll find each of these experiences unpleasant—and all of them together might be downright miserable. You can get instant relief from all of them by getting a cigarette and lighting it up—but this runs counter to what it was you wanted to get done in your life, quitting smoking. Under these circumstances, you have a choice: accept the experiences that come with not smoking, or avoid them by lighting up. When you do stuff in order to escape or stop feeling a certain way—bingo. You've got experiential avoidance.

Acceptance Isn't Approving, Wanting, or Liking

Let's get clear on something: by acceptance, we absolutely don't mean approval, desire, or fondness. There's a significant difference between being willing to have an experience, and wishing for it or enjoying it when it happens.

If you really want to smoke a cigarette but choose not to, you may feel jumpy, cranky, or agitated. If you want to take a plane trip, and you're anxious about flying, the rumble of the engines and the chimes that sound after takeoff might scare the wits out of you. Neither is a fun way to spend an afternoon, and any attempts on your part to make them so will probably result in failure and frustration.

> ...there was never yet philosopher that could endure the toothache patiently...
>
> —Shakespeare, *Much Ado About Nothing*, Act V, Scene 1

Acceptance, as we mean it, is independent of desire and judgment, and this includes both positive and negative judgments. When you accept a particular experience, you acknowledge it, stay present to it, and take it in without attempting to alter it in any way. You don't have much control over what thoughts come up after that: You might very well react negatively: "I don't like it!" But a negative reaction doesn't equal experiential avoidance, which demands that you act to reduce, eliminate, or control your experiences.

This might sound similar to what we said in the last chapter about the typically fruitless struggle to change the content of your thoughts: all the effort in the world probably won't get you very far. But thinking about Lester is very different from getting in the car and driving to Albuquerque to pay him a visit. Efforts you put into acceptance are things you can *do,* and these can make significant contributions to your psychological flexibility.

Acceptance Isn't Just Gritting Your Teeth and Bearing It, Either

We're not going to get up on a soapbox and start preaching about the evils of our feel-good culture, but we do have to admit it: acceptance is pretty hard to sell these days. We live in a place where discomfort is regularly shunned and suffering is routinely avoided. And we live in a time when escaping from difficult experiences is as easy as making a trip to the pharmacy or the liquor cabinet. Since we're sold on the idea that you should decide where you want to go in life and then head off in that direction, even if that means feeling some pain along the way, we can sound kind of stoic at times. To some extent, this is unavoidable. We wouldn't need to write about it if we were talking about the acceptance of kittens and rainbows. On the other hand, we're not talking about grim resignation either. Acceptance isn't about giving up; it's about opening up—to possibilities, alternatives, and the fringe benefits that sometimes come with really hard experiences.

Game: Silver Mining
Props: None • **Difficulty:** Easy

Cyclists know that climbing hills is a pain—literally. You stomp on the pedals, strain, and ache. And the hill just keeps coming. Sometimes you can't even see the top, or worse, sometimes you can. But on all but the most perverse of hills, there's a carrot waiting at the top of the climb: a fast descent down the back side that's one of the closest things to flying human beings can experience.

In this game, you'll think of a situation in which you either did open up or could have opened up to some kind of painful experience. Your objective is to just sit with that memory and let your awareness nibble around its edges. Your objective is to make contact with something lovely that you either might have missed or did miss by avoiding pain—a little piece of silver in a lot of gray. Give yourself a good ten minutes to roll the experience around in your head. There are extra points in it for you if the silver spot you find leads you to appreciate someone or something more than you did before you started. Another thing that's good for extra credit it to find something precious to you that was a consequence of genuine disaster. It's actually pretty easy to find precious moments in situations where you were anxious about something that never came to pass. But what if you worried about something that really did go terribly, horribly wrong? Sometimes there are little treasures to be found even in those kinds of ashes, if you're willing to sift through them.

Consider:

- *"I was incredibly nervous about going to that dinner party, and I did get blind drunk and make a perfect ass of myself. But if I had skipped it, I never would have met Allan…"*

- *"Mispronouncing 'mitochondrion' in biology class and getting laughed at by everyone was awful, but when my daughter came home from school crying about something similar, I knew exactly how she felt. We really connected that day."*

- *"I worried for months that the Collins deal would turn out to be a bust and that I'd catch hell for it. And that's how it actually turned out—and they fired me. It hurt like hell, but it got me back into veterinary school, and now I feel like I'm going to be able to do work that matters to me."*

The Cost of Avoidance

Lenny Bruce said that the truth is what is, and Jesus said that the truth will make you free. The two of them point us toward the idea that by willingly and openly engaging with what *is*, we're liberated to imagine and move toward what might be. When we decide that something must not or should not be—"I mustn't be uncomfortable riding in an elevator," "I can't allow myself to seem stupid in front of my peers"—we take away some of our options for living. Our world gets just a little bit smaller. Over a lifetime, avoidance of what *is* can confine us to very small places. The cost of persistent avoidance can be great indeed.

When you designate some experiences as unacceptable, you begin to establish the edges of the world you're willing to inhabit. As your world gets smaller and smaller, the options you have for living in a way that matters to you grow fewer and fewer.

The Upside of Avoidance

We want to say a quick word about how there's a time and place for avoidance. We've consistently made the point that there's nothing inherently bad about acting out the "problem" or negative sides of the various process areas—unless doing so specifically gets in between you and the life you want to live. Avoidance is no exception to this rule.

It's one thing to lose yourself in the poster of the alpine scene on the ceiling of the dentist's office, to take a Valium before your appointment, or to accept the nitrous oxide when it's offered. It's another thing entirely to put off getting that root canal until you're reduced to taking your meals through a straw because you can't stand the prospect of hearing the drill and being confined to the dentist's chair for two hours.

So how do you tell the difference? When is avoiding an experience a reasonable choice for catering to your comfort, and when is it a problem that works to diminish your psychological flexibility? The answer lies in whether the avoidant act gets in the way of something that matters to you, something that, if pursued, would get you closer to someplace you want to be. And, from an ACT perspective, your values orient you in the direction of where you want to be. Often in the book, we've brought the issue back to the central idea of valued living. In the next chapter, we'll dig deeper into the meaning of values in ACT.

6

Meaning
Matters:
Values

For what is a man, what has he got?

If not himself, then he has naught.

To say the things he truly feels;

And not the words of one who kneels.

The record shows

I took the blows—

And did it my way!

—Paul Anka (sung by Frank Sinatra), "My Way"

One of the hassles of living our lives in the stream of time is that we're biased toward believing that much of the world works in a linear fashion. We're born, we live, and we die. We matriculate at school, study, and graduate. Planes take off, cruise, and land. Books have a first and a last page, and they're set up to be the most comprehensible if you read them in the traditional fashion, from the first chapter to the last, one page at a time. This book is no exception, really.

Despite this, it's a conceptual challenge to organize the six process areas into a straight line, one chapter after the other. The reality of the areas' interaction is much more circular, fluid, shifting, and evolving. Within the ACT professional community, the six process areas are graphically represented as points on a hexagon, a diagram that's known as the *hexaflex*. We haven't made much of this diagram, since in this book we've really wanted to focus on the everyday ideas that emerge from this work rather than on the ways psychologists talk about it. But if you look at an example of the diagram, you can see a graphic interpretation of how each process area is connected to the others.

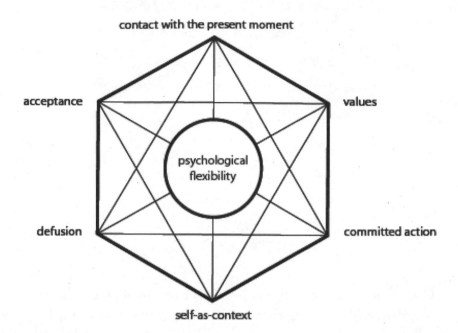

The Hexaflex Model

As we consider this work, we can see how each of the areas is expressed in the others, but sometimes it's hard to understand the more nuanced points of a process without having a sense of how the others work within it. Nowhere is this truer than with values, the ACT process we'll discuss in this chapter. We've decided to work up to this chapter, but we certainly could have started with it.

Before you go on, we should acknowledge that there really won't be much talk about anxiety, per se, in this chapter. The issue of values and the role they play in our lives is relevant to the whole of your experience, not just that part that's encumbered by anxiety. As we'll see, values are the things that can guide us through difficult experiences like anxiety. They dignify and provide the incentive for the rest of the sometimes-difficult work that's described in this book. So for the rest of this chapter, excuse us for not specifically orienting all of our experiences to anxiety.

A Reason to Get Up in the Morning

As you've read to this point, you've seen phrases like "a life that matters to you," "valued living," and "a rich and purposeful life," used again and again. All of these phrases point back to the values process. Values direct the difficult work we do in ACT. Make no mistake about it: Sitting calmly and attentively through a moment of fear is hard. Stepping back from a well-rehearsed thought about how you aren't smart enough or good enough is hard. Accepting feelings of panic is hard. To do any of these things just to get rid of some feeling or to comply with someone else's idea of what it means to be normal or healthy borders on the masochistic. When we do these hard things in the service of a value, though, our hard work seems justified.

Values set us off in a particular direction in life, and as we head in that direction, obstacles emerge. When these are obstacles in the world, they define some of our life tasks. We value being part of a loving family, so we connect with our relations, seek out partners, and work to build our homes. We value education and learning, so we search for teachers and apply ourselves to the task of studying. We value productive work, so we find employers or develop business opportunities we find in the world.

When these obstacles are inside of us—thoughts, emotions, and the like—they define a different sort of life task. From an ACT perspective, the tasks are organized around the other process areas. We are tasked with being open and accepting, with keeping our focus gently in the present, with holding our thoughts lightly, and so forth.

Values from an ACT Perspective

In everyday speech, "values" can take on a fairly wide range of meanings, depending on who's using the word and where she falls within a number of psychological, philosophical, and spiritual traditions. When the word pops up in the popular media, especially in the context of cultural or political discussions, it can be very loaded—divisive, prescriptive, and even sometimes accusatory. In ACT, though, we use the word in a fairly restricted way. For this reason, we've opted not to offer a simple definition of the term right from the start of our discussion, as we've done with the other process terms. Instead, we'll walk you through what we mean, exactly, when we talk about values in ACT.

You Get to Pick 'Em

Frank Sinatra said it when he famously sang the song, a line from which is the epigraph to this chapter: he did it *his* way—not his mother's way, his country's way, a way he read about in some book or the other. He made a choice. He did it his way. We may listen to our parents, the culture, and the wise, but ultimately, we get to choose our own direction in life. It's not always easy, but it's always possible.

Values, from an ACT perspective, are choices that we deliberately and consciously make about the directions we want to go in our lives. Here we specifically distinguish between choices and feelings, emotions, and thoughts.

While you might have very strong feelings about your values, your values are not themselves feelings. The key to this distinction is that, while you can actively construct your values, you have little or no conscious control over your feelings. In some ways, you can think of the construction of values like the construction of a house. Feelings, emotions, and thoughts, on the other hand, are more like the weather where the house is built. Some days it's sunny, and on others, it rains. You might be able to identify patterns in the weather over time—it's cold in January and hot in July—but you don't get to choose whether the sun comes out at any given moment. Your house will certainly be affected by the weather to which it is subjected. But if the wind blows down your fence, you get to freely make the choice of whether to tear it out or rebuild it. What you do with your values "house" is up to you.

But let's not stretch the building metaphor any closer to its point of collapse. To use a specific example that illustrates the distinction between thought and emotion as values, as opposed to choices that we make, think for a moment about racial prejudice. If you were raised in the United States (or many other places), you've grown up in a culture in which it's more accurate to ask "In what ways am I racist?" than to ask "Am I racist?" Our culture (if you're American, and perhaps even if you're not) carries the baggage of racial oppression, and it takes a very long time for deeply ingrained prejudices like this to change. Even when we personally value the practice of equality and abhor the idea of discrimination, we are likely to still carry some of the seeds of these prejudices.

For just about all of us, even the thought of the unabashed, publicly sanctioned discrimination of years past is repugnant. The evidence of racial hatred and violence we see in the world today is even more so. But in our unguarded moments, how many of us can claim to be free from the influence of racially influenced thinking? When someone cuts us off on the highway, when we're walking alone at night, or when police lights flash behind us—where do our thoughts rush? The specific answer to this question isn't as important as recognizing the distinction between what we think and feel, and what we elect, freely and consciously, to do. Being susceptible to racist thoughts and feelings doesn't in any way preclude us from choosing the value of racial equality even when our feelings, thoughts, and emotions go their own way.

A great many of our most deeply held values are like this. In electing these values over the course of a whole lifetime—to be a loving and caring parent, to be a faithful and nurturing spouse, to be a kind and compassionate person—we set the bar very high for ourselves. As we'll see later, in the chapter about commitment, sometimes we succeed in furthering our values, and sometimes we don't. Sometimes it gives us pleasure to live in a way that furthers our values. Sometimes it causes us terrific pain. Sometimes we think that valued living is wonderful, and sometimes we think it stinks. However, we can always *choose* to pursue a valued direction regardless of what we think and feel about doing so. Part of our deeply held values is likely to be a certain steadfastness in the face of difficulties, which are certain to arise both from outside, in the world, and from inside ourselves.

They're Complete in and of Themselves

In 1923, the *New York Times* asked explorer George Mallory why he was so keen on climbing Mount Everest, to which he supposedly made the famous reply, "Because it's there." If Mallory was telling the truth, he wasn't in the mountain-climbing business for the fame, the fortune, or to impress the ladies. Rather, we can imagine that there was some match between what he wanted his life to be about and reaching the top of the world's highest peak. Mallory found reason enough to climb the mountain in the simple fact that he chose to do so. In some way, values are like that, and the reason why is rather interesting.

Behavioral scientists talk about *punishers* and *reinforcers*. Take some living thing—a human, a rat, or what have you—put it in a certain environment, and then identify some behavior it might engage in. A reinforcer is some change in that environment that, when it occurs, makes that behavior more likely to occur. On the other hand, a punisher is a change that, when it occurs, will make that behavior less likely. Say, for example, you put a rat in a cage equipped with a lever. If the rat pushes the lever and a sunflower seed drops down for it to eat, chances are that the rat will push the lever more frequently. This is a reinforcer for the rat's lever pushing. If the rat pushes the lever and—zap!—it gets shocked, the rodent will learn pretty quickly not to push the lever. The electric jolt is a punisher.

Behavioral reinforcers for nonhumans are pretty straightforward. There's not a long list of them: food, shelter, sex, social contact, and so forth, as well as associated things. The list of punishers for nonhumans is correspondingly short. The rat likes to eat sunflower seeds, and it doesn't like to get shocked. But how would our cage experiment work if, when the rat pushed the lever, we honored it or said nice things about its fur? How would it work if each time the rat pushed the lever, a group of scientists gathered at the back of the room to whisper about how it was a nasty, mean-spirited spreader of disease?

Exactly right. It wouldn't work well at all. A rat will work for food and to avoid pain. Humans will too, but we'll also work for all sorts of other stuff, much of which is downout silly and, all of which we've pretty much just made up over the years: the Nobel Prize, the league record for rebounds, the Employee of the Year award, and so forth. Reinforcement works differently for humans than it does for nonhumans. The extent of this difference is beyond the scope of this book, but at least it's worth mentioning that this has something to do with our ability to use language to relate to the world. Nonhumans need to experience the consequences of actions in a fairly direct way in order for these actions to influence behavior. Human behavior, on the other hand, can be reinforced indirectly through language as well as directly through experience. None of us, for example, has directly experienced heaven, yet the promise of an eternal reward after death can generate a lot of behavior for some people.

Values, from an ACT perspective, create a special kind of reinforcer. Some behaviors are only reinforced if they produce something. Putting a dollar in the soda machine is only reinforced if soda comes out. Leaving a message for a colleague is only reinforced if that person, at least sometimes, returns your calls. But values involve a different kind of reinforcer.

When we construct a value, we make some decisions about the kinds of behaviors that are consistent with that value. After that, the chance to engage in the behavior is reinforcing all by itself. For example, if you've chosen to value being a good parent, you might decide that consistently spending your free time with your children is something that good parents do. This decision might not, in actual practice, be very convenient for you. You might miss out on a lot of enjoyable things that you could do alone. And, especially as they get older, your children might not act especially grateful for the extra attention you pay them. But if you choose to be a good parent and decide that good parents spend abundant time with their children, spending time with them will be worthwhile even though doing so sometimes produces outcomes you like and sometimes not. When your children grow up, they will have grown up with someone who made time for them—and for your purposes, this is consistent with the value you find in being a good parent.

For a more dramatic example, recall Viktor Frankl's experience in the death camps of Nazi Germany. With starvation, brutality, sickness, and death abounding, it would be hard to point to any direct benefits Frankl enjoyed because of his decision to remain in the camp rather than escape. The reinforcer for his choice to stay behind with his patients was the intrinsic match between his decision and his own construction of what it meant to be both a good doctor and a moral human being. And the profound sense of liberation he felt upon making that choice hints at the power these chosen values have to add to the depth and richness of our experience, even under the most difficult circumstances.

They Change and Grow Along with Us

We've been talking a lot about what values are. Now let's spend a little time talking about what they're not.

Values aren't goals. Basically, if you can achieve, earn, attain, or complete it, it's not a value—it's a goal. In the greater context of living out your values, goals are very important. In our ACT work, though, goals are set according to the values they serve. If you value learning, your value might serve you through a lifetime of setting goals: a high-school diploma, a bachelor's degree, a graduate degree; a foreign language learned in adulthood; your first read through *Remembrance of Things Past* or *Ulysses*. When will you have learned enough? The answer to this question is, of course, entirely up to you, but it's at least possible that the value you place on learning could provide direction for your whole life, through many individual goals.

Another thing values are not is fixed. Values evolve with us. They're dynamic. The kinds of things that further our values change over time. Consider parenting: What's involved in being a good parent to a newborn? To a teenager? To an adult? A parent who turns a toddler loose in a crowded shopping mall to find his own way and socialize with his diapered friends gets taken away in handcuffs. And for the parent who swaddles her teenager and pushes her around the mall in a stroller—a straitjacket. Reverse the ages of the children, though, and the situations would be very different, with both adults probably living out the value of being a good parent.

Game: Digging Down into Your Values
Props: A pen and paper, timer for the speed round • **Difficulty:** Medium

Enough talk about values. Let's actually make contact with them! This game is broken up into two rounds: a speed round and a challenge round.

Start by making a game card by drawing a simple table on some paper. Draw some rough lines to mark off ten rows and three columns. Label the columns as follows:

Value   ·   Importance   Action

Then, on the left, label the rows with ten areas in which you might find value:

family, friends, work, learning,
fun, spirituality, community, fitness,
the environment, and beauty.

Don't worry about figuring out what each of these areas "should" mean. They'll take on some meaning for you as you write them, and this is exactly the meaning we intended.

Speed round: With your grid in front of you, set your timer for twenty minutes. This allows two minutes for you to consider each of these value areas. As soon as you start the timer, take a look at the first area: family. Let yourself wonder about the role this area plays in your life. Watch as whatever thoughts come up. Now look to the columns on the right. In the first, the one labeled "importance," rate this value area according to how important you feel it is in your life. Use 1 to mean "not very important: something that doesn't play much of a role in my life" and 10 to be "very important: one of my most deeply held values," with the other numbers meaning something along that range. Don't obsess over what, exactly, each number means. Remember, you only have twenty minutes to finish. Now switch to the next column, the one labeled "action." Using a similar scale, record a score that indicates how you feel about your actions in this area. In this case, let 1 mean "I'm concerned about this; I would like to really do a lot more here," and 10 mean "I'm all over it; I'm very happy with my efforts in this area." When you're done with the family area, move on to friends. Continue until you finish all ten areas. (If your timer goes off before you finish, you'll just have to cheat and finish anyway. But you'll know...)

Challenge round: Now that you have your grid filled out and the timer is off, it's time to challenge yourself to make sense out of what you have on the paper. Look at the numbers. Do they make sense to you? Do you see any patterns that would indicate that you might be spending too little time on some of the areas of your life that are important to you? To finish this round and the game, ask yourself the following questions, taking as much time as you need to come up with your answers:

- If I could only work on five of these areas, which would they be?

- If I could only work on three of these areas, which would they be?

- If I could only work on one of these areas, which one would it be?

After you finish this game, you might want to keep your game card. Spending some time with it might open you up to the question of values in your life. If this game was very difficult for you, especially if you had a hard time answering questions you put to yourself about values, read on. There are some interesting parallels between our values and the things in life that cause us distress—like anxiety—that can offer clues about what you really want your life to be about.

The Dark Side of Values—Sort Of

We've come to the part in our discussion where we warn you not to get caught up in the details of the process for no good reason. We keep hammering at this point in each process area because we're single-mindedly committed to helping you see ACT as a means to liberation rather than as a new and different kind of prison.

Remember how we said that there was nothing inherently good about keeping in contact with the present moment, remaining defused from thoughts, or practicing acceptance? Or, on the other hand, nothing inherently bad about floating off into the past or future, becoming totally absorbed in a thought, or engaging in a little avoidance every now and again? In each of these cases, we pointed to valued living as the measure of the situation. As long as what you're doing isn't keeping you away from what you want your life to be about, knock yourself out.

It's a little different with values. Sure, you might allow that doing things contrary to your values might be all right from time to time, but since values are evolving *patterns* of behavior, the odd lapse just gets folded into the whole. A few nights of eating a second helping of dessert in the context of a pattern of behavior based on your value of health and fitness isn't much to write home about.

The "dark side" of values, if there is one, can be found in the kinds of breakdowns they tend to provoke in some of the other process areas—fusion and avoidance being the two in particular to watch for. Want to see fusion and avoidance? Start talking about values. Do you value being a good partner in your relationship? Here comes the fusion:

- "A good husband should…"

- "I can't be a good girlfriend unless I…"

- "All couples do that! We must…"

- "When I'm in a relationship, I always…"

- "We can't make that work. I'm just the kind of person who…"

And the avoidance isn't far behind. You know that thing he does? That thing that drives you crazy? More than crazy: sometimes it makes you want to leave? You know you need to talk to him about it, but if you even mention it, he'll hit the roof. So you put it off—again.

So fusion and avoidance often pop up around values. Fortunately, you've very recently read about some ways to deal with fusion and avoidance. One useful thing about this common co-occurrence is that fusion and avoidance often act as a kind of "value sign," a big red "X" that marks the spot where you'll find something you care about. Look for fusion and avoidance, and what are you more than likely to find behind them? A value. Why? Because our values and vulnerabilities are poured from the same vessel. We feel the most vulnerable in areas that matter to us.

There's no mystery why this is so. There isn't much chance that you'll get caught up in a thought or avoid an unpleasant experience—heck, even *have* an unpleasant experience—in relation to some area of your life that just doesn't matter to you all that much. If you couldn't care less about your sporting abilities and someone laughs at your fumbling backhand or inept golf swing, you'll probably join in on the joke. But if you've spent a lot of time and energy to become a champion on the courts or the courses, these comments are likely to smart—and you're likely to do the kinds of things that hurt or scared people do when they're in pain, like engage in fusion and avoidance.

Game: Claiming Your Mountain
Props: A mirror for round 1, a recording device for round 2, another person for round 3 •
Difficulty: Hard

Want to watch fusion and avoidance bubble up around a value? This is the game for you. To prepare for round 1, think about something that matters to you, a value that you hold. Come up with some statement that sums up what really engaging in this value would look like. There's no end to the possibilities:

- "I want to be a great mom."

- "More than anything, I want to be a really amazing husband."

- "Rocks are my life. I want to be the best geologist I can be."

You get the idea. Now, with that statement in mind, get ready to play the game. Follow the rules for each round. Go very slowly, and pay close attention to what comes up for you in each.

Round 1: Take out your mirror (or stand in front of it, if it's on the floor or mounted on the wall). Look yourself in the eye and, in a loud, clear voice, say your value statement out loud.

Round 2: Set up your recording device (laptops are great for this kind of thing). Recording your voice or, better yet, your image on video, say your value statement out loud, once again, in a clear and confident voice. Once you've made your recording, listen to it several times.

Round 3: This one is the best, of course. Sit down with the person you've found to play with you. Look that person in the eye and say your value statement out loud.

Round 4: Now go back and listen again. Listen while watching your own face. Listen again with compassion for that person you hear in the audio or see in the video. Listen with your eyes closed and see if you can hear the depth of meaning in that commitment.

If your mind chatters, let it. There's something at stake here that's more important than what your mind thinks on any given day. Ask yourself this question: if you could decide to live out either your thoughts or your values, which would you choose?

The object of the game is not to try to convince yourself or to repeat positive affirmations over and over. It's a serious test of your willingness and acceptance. Did you find that you could own whatever came up? What did you feel as you played through each round? A bit of constriction? A bit of reluctance? A bit of hesitation? Right now, answer this question to yourself: would you play the game again in this very moment with a different value? How many areas of your life are there about which you would be willing to declare, in front of witnesses, your intention to truly excel—whatever that means?

Tough, isn't it? And have you noticed that what we've been asking here is that you just *say* what it is that you want to do really splendidly in your life? We haven't mentioned anything about *doing*—with all of the challenges and obstacles that both your mind and the world will put in your path. The actual work of making values into everyday experience takes commitment. Fortunately, commitment is the subject of our next discussion.

7

Thou

Art

Peter:

Commitment

All of old. Nothing else ever. Ever tried. Ever failed. No matter.

Try again. Fail again. Fail better.

—Samuel Beckett, *Worstward Ho*

So far we've talked about four of the six ACT process areas: in ordinary words, these processes are living in and for the present moment, holding our thoughts lightly, accepting the sweet and the sad, and choosing a life that matters to us. The fifth area we're going to talk about is commitment.

Commitment, from an ACT perspective, is the act of making a solemn and irrevocable promise to do all of the things we've talked about so far in this book from now on, forever, without ever missing a step or making a mistake. In this chapter, we'll ask you to stand up in front of your family, friends, and coworkers and declare out loud your resolution to live in a way that realizes your deepest values...

Wait, wait! Before you throw the book across the room—we're kidding! If you've been with us since the beginning of the book, you know we aren't being serious. But as you read the paragraph above, did you felt a little twinge somewhere? Did you? An uneasy feeling, maybe a little bit of terror. Commitment? That's scary stuff. If you didn't have a problem with anxiety, being asked to make a commitment like the one we described above would be more than enough to give you one. In the last chapter, we discussed how thinking and talking about what you value can lead to fusion and avoidance. If that's true of values, it's doubly so for commitment.

Everyday Commitment

So what do we mean when we talk about commitment from an ACT point of view? Let's hold that thought for a moment and, instead, talk about what we mean when we talk about commitment in the everyday, ordinary sense.

When we use the word in our day-to-day conversations, we typically take commitment to mean "a promise we make to do something in the future." Some of these promises are related to single acts or combinations of acts that are limited in scope, kind of like the goals we discussed in the last chapter. Of course, just because these kinds of commitments are fixed to specific, limited goals doesn't mean that they're easy or trivial. They might, in fact, be very complex and difficult: becoming a doctor, reaching the summit of Aconcagua, establishing a homeless shelter in your community. But even if these goal-focused commitments are heroic in scope, they can still be honored by achieving a certain outcome.

Identifying these kinds of goal-focused commitments in our lives is pretty easy. We commit to pick up the kids from soccer. We commit to make monthly payments on an installment loan. We commit to bring the green gelatin salad with the pineapple chunks and the little marshmallows to Saturday's potluck. For the most part, it's also easy to understand these kinds of commitments in the context of our lives: you either honor them or you don't, and consequences follow in either case. The kids make it home after the game, and you enjoy the peace of mind of knowing they're safe: check. The loan payment never gets made, and the bank tows away the station wagon: check. All of the guests at the party stare warily at your glistening green blob. Finally, someone pokes at it with a spoon: check.

Other promises we make about the future aren't fixed on discrete goals. Sometimes we make commitments that can only be honored with ongoing patterns of behavior. We commit to love, honor, and cherish our spouses. We commit to being good parents. We commit to taking care of our health, to exercising and eating healthfully. Do you see the connection between these kinds of commitments and the values we discussed in chapter 6? These more open-ended commitments are a means of translating values into life. In this way the process areas of values and commitment, as we understand them from an ACT perspective, are reflected vividly in each other.

The making of values-focused commitments is perilous business, especially if we take commitment in the everyday sense of promised actions for the future. In contrast to goal-focused commitments, making sense of the open-ended values commitment in the context of our lives requires some effort.

Committing to the Unknowable

In the everyday sense, we make these kinds of values commitments all the time. And we also break them—all the time. For some of us, the uncertainty about whether we'll honor these kinds of commitments over time is a significant source of anxiety.

Game: Checking in on Your Commitments
Props: None • **Difficulty:** Easy, and perhaps troubling

In this game, you'll start by thinking of a values-focused commitment you've made. Once you have it in mind, the game proceeds in three rounds.

Call to mind your commitment. You only need to think of one, but be specific. It'll probably come easily to you. If it takes a while, just breathe gently and wait for it to show up.

Round 1: Once you've got your commitment pictured clearly in your mind, let yourself wonder about how it might play out in your life in a week, a month, a year, and five years, if the events of your life go as you intend. What would it look like if you honored this commitment in ten years' time?

Round 2: Now take a deep breath, hold it, and let it out slowly. Start letting images gather in your mind of what your life would start to look like if you *didn't* honor your commitment. What would your life look like in a decade if you discovered that you weren't able to keep this commitment or if you just decided to walk away from it? Be careful. Your tendency will probably be to try to rescue or advise your future self. Don't do it. Just wonder about what breaking your commitment would be like; don't solve any problems you encounter or try to push away anything that comes up.

Round 3: Now take one more deep breath and let it out. This time, consider your life as it is right now and where, to the best of your knowledge, you see it heading in the future. Let yourself wonder *whether* you'll keep your commitment. Don't try too hard to argue for one outcome or the other. Just wonder what might actually happen. Do you think you'll honor your commitment, or will you let it go? In this last round in particular, pay very close attention to the sensations you feel in your body.

Of the three rounds, which seemed to cause the most noticeable changes in your body? Was it the third? If it was, there's a good reason. Think back to our discussion in chapter 2, about our tendency to be ill at ease with ambiguity. When we make these kinds of open-ended, values-focused commitments, we always open the door to ambiguity. Will you honor your commitment? Unless you have a crystal ball (and know how to make it work), your honest answer to this question is "I don't know." And the bad news is that, as long as you're still breathing, your answer will be either "I don't know" or "No, I failed." With open-ended commitments, ambiguity is a certainty, and you can only get relief from this ambiguity in failure.

Consider someone with an alcohol problem. After years of problem drinking, she finally decides to make a change. She goes into rehab. She gets the best education about alcoholism and its treatment. She assembles a team of doctors, therapists, good friends, and loved ones to support her through recovery.

And then she makes a promise to herself: I'm not going to take another drink.

Will she drink again? We don't know. And as long as she's still breathing, we'll never know—and neither will she. We might talk about the odds of her relapse, based on the success rates of the treatments she receives. We might look at examples of commitments she has made in the past and make a guess about her commitment "credit score." But the only way to "answer" the question of whether she'll drink again is to watch each unfolding moment of her life—from now until she draws her last breath—to see whether she'll open another bottle or raise another glass to her lips. Depending on circumstances, we could be watching this process for a very long time. And all the while, we'll be swimming in—you guessed it—ambiguity. Many people in recovery struggle with this not-knowing, and there's more than a little reason to suppose that this struggle is behind many a relapse: In the moment when she takes that next drink, the ambiguity goes away. We get our answer: yes, she will drink again. And in that answer, even if it's devastating, she gets a moment of peace.

Commitment in ACT

By now, you probably smell a rat. We've devoted a whole chapter to commitment, and we've already told you that committed action is one of the fundamental processes that makes ACT work. But now we have all this business about ambiguity and the anxiety that comes with making promises about the future. So, what gives?

You're right to be suspicious. It turns out that there's more to commitment, from an ACT perspective, than just making promises about the future. While the everyday sense of the word is certainly a part of commitment in ACT, it doesn't tell the whole story.

Looking to the Future, Acting in the Present

If it were common for us to always keep the promises we make to ourselves and others about our actions in the future, our commitments would be effectively synonymous with our values. There wouldn't really be a need for this chapter. You could just read chapter 6, spend some time deciding what you want your life to be about, and then—poof! You'd be golden.

But we all know this isn't the case. The narratives of our lives are made up of story after story of broken promises, of honest commitments made today that become soul-crushing burdens tomorrow, of our best-laid plans going terribly, horribly awry. Whether these setbacks are due to circumstances beyond our control or our own inability to live up to the expectations we set for ourselves is beside the point. Whatever its cause, failure is a familiar friend to us all. And so commitments—in the everyday sense of the word, as promises we make about the future—aren't likely to lead us to greater psychological flexibility.

But what if we were less concerned with the outcome of these promises we make? What if we understood commitment as something that we do in the present? Consider again our friend who's trying to overcome alcohol addiction. Will she drink again? As we said, we don't know. Only time will tell. We can't answer that question, but there are others we can answer: Is she drinking now? Right now? No. And what about now? Still no. Moment by moment, she can commit to this value that she's chasing.

The understanding of commitment that interests us is committing to act in the present moment in ways that are directed by values and perhaps are aimed at goals. We're less concerned with whether we achieve those goals. It's fine if we do, but it's not the whole story. This is because, sometimes (and maybe oftentimes), we can't really imagine what's possible in our lives. Have you ever known someone who really turned his life around? Someone who went from rock bottom to a life that he was delighted with?

You can imagine such a situation even if you can't think of anyone off the top of your head. Again, consider our friend who's wrestling with a drinking problem. If we took a look at her life, let's say, five years ago, she might be waking up on the floor most nights. She may be in and out of abusive relationships and unable to hold a job for very long. Maybe she wraps her car around a tree some rainy evening. At this point in her life, what do you suppose she might hope for? Is it perhaps the case that the most she can let herself think possible is that she might—just might—be alive at the same time next year?

Now jump ahead ten years. Let's say she really turns her life around. She falls in with some people who help her kick her drinking problem. They set her up in a job in the mail room of an import-export company. Over the years, she works her way out of the mail room and into the sales department. Eventually, she's promoted to manage a team of salespeople based in China. She finds herself in the business class of a jetliner, flying from Los Angeles to Beijing. She's wiping her hands on a hot towel; flight attendants are offering her sparkling mineral water and extra pillows.

To go from skid row to business class, our friend would have to beat some pretty steep odds. But stories like hers are not unheard of by any means. When she was trying to make it to the next year, though, do you suppose she was dreaming of hot towels and sparkling water thirty-five thousand feet over the Pacific? Chances are she wasn't. Life is often like that: we can only see so far ahead, and to be able to imagine the possibilities once we've reached a certain future point, we sometimes need to just move off in that direction and see what happens next.

We just don't know how things will turn out much of the time. This being the case, the outcomes of our commitments, whether they're to limited goals or evolving values, aren't something we have a lot of control over. But moment to moment, we can commit to doing something that will get us a little closer to whatever it is that matters to us. And when we fail—and we *will* fail—we'll suddenly find ourselves in a new moment where, once again, we can commit to our valued lives. It's in this turning back where you'll find the heart of commitment in ACT.

> And I say also unto thee that thou art Peter, and upon this rock I will build my church; and the gates of hell shall not prevail against it. And I will give unto thee the keys of the kingdom of heaven; and whatsoever thou shalt bind on earth shall be bound in heaven; and whatsoever thou shalt loose on earth shall be loosed in heaven.
>
> —Matthew 16:18–19

Strong Walls Can Rest on a Shaky Foundation

There's a story in the Bible that points at the understanding of commitment we're arguing for. It's the story of Peter, first among the apostles, the "rock" on which Jesus declares he'll build his church. It's also the story of Peter, the undependable, unfaithful, and short-tempered fisherman. These two people are one and the same—and this matters for the purpose of our discussion of commitment. (And just so we're clear: we relate this only because we love it. It's a beautiful description of what it means to be committed to something even though we're all too human and fallible. This isn't Sunday school, and we're not preachers—just a couple of guys hooked on a story.)

It all starts when Jesus comes upon Simon Peter, his brother, and a couple of other fishermen, plying their trade on the shores of the Sea of Galilee. In most of the gospels, Peter decides to join up with Jesus after Jesus promises to make him a "fisher of men" (for example, see Matt. 4:18–19). In the Gospel of Luke, though, Peter is talked into apostlehood only when the Messiah offers him a professional tip that directs him to "a great multitude of fishes" (Luke 5:6). This is the start of a roller-coaster relationship that winds its way through Judea.

In the Gospel of Matthew, Peter accompanies Jesus when he walks on water, only to lose faith at the last minute and go splashing down into the drink (Matt. 14:28–31). During the last supper, Jesus foretells his own death and warns that, with him gone, the apostles' faith will be shaken. "Though all may have their faith in you shaken," Peter brays, "mine will never be" (Matt. 26:23), making a characteristic promise-about-the-future commitment. Jesus, indulgent, replies that not only will Peter's faith be shaken, but he will also actually commit three acts of betrayal even before the night is over (Matt. 26:34). But before we can see how the betrayal part of the story plays out, Jesus up and takes Peter and some of the other disciples off to the garden of Gethsemane. The Messiah asks Peter and his fellows to keep watch. Jesus goes into the garden to pray, but when he comes back, he finds Peter and the others sound asleep (Matt. 26:40), leading Jesus to remark that "the spirit is willing, but the flesh is weak" (Matt. 26.41). As if that weren't bad enough, Peter can't even stay awake a second time or even a third—making the whole agony-in-the-garden thing pretty much a bust for Peter.

When the priests and Pharisees, acting on a tip from Judas, come to arrest Jesus, Peter is once again in rare form. In the Gospel of John, as Jesus is taken into custody, Peter loses his temper, draws his sword, and hacks the ear off of the high priest's servant, some poor schlub named Malchus. Again, Jesus gently rebukes him, and the story continues.

While Jesus is questioned, Peter sulks off into the street and snuggles up to a warm fire. It doesn't take too long for a servant girl to recognize the first of the disciples. And here come the betrayals: *Uh, no. You must be mistaking me for someone else* (Mark 14:68). Not satisfied, she repeats her charge to the others gathered around, to which Peter responds something like: *Jesus? Never met the guy* (Mark 14:70).

Finally, the people around the fire get wise: *You* so *have a Galilean accent! It's not as if there are that many Galileans kicking around Jerusalem. You* must *be friends with this Jesus guy.*

Caught, Peter does what many of us might do: he blows his stack, swears like a sailor (or maybe a fisherman?), and denies any knowledge of his master: "I know not this man of whom ye speak" (Mark 14:71).

Then comes the grim day of the Crucifixion and the mystery of the Resurrection. Despite all of his shady behavior, Jesus still reveals himself to Peter several times. On the last occasion, he asks the disciple three times, "Do you love me?" (John 21:15–17). And each time Peter insists that he does. And so Jesus holds open the door to his disciple one more time: "Follow thou me" (John 21:22).

There's a lovely message in this story. It's an acknowledgment that none of us is perfect. We have short tempers, bad moods, moments of faithlessness—and yet, as long as we're above ground, we have a chance to turn back to what matters to us. Betrayal after betrayal, outburst after outburst—and Peter still comes back. It's not necessarily as important that Jesus welcomes him—although this gives the story a much happier ending. What matters is that, each time he wandered, Peter turned back.

The Heart of Commitment in ACT

We think this turning back is at the heart of the commitment process in ACT. We choose our values and we transform them from words into deeds with commitment: *I will be a good mother to my daughter, I will be kind, I will excel in my profession.* Sure, we make promises about the future—and we fail. We fail often. We fail spectacularly. It's hard, if not impossible, to imagine a value of any significance that anyone could succeed in furthering all the time. The most loving parent is occasionally self-absorbed and unavailable to his child. The most dedicated professor sometimes blows off her students. Saint Augustine pleaded with God to make him chaste and constant—just not yet. Achievement is wonderful, but perseverance is at the heart of commitment.

Game: The Well-Stocked Pantry
Props: None • **Difficulty:** Easy

This short game is kind of a warm-up to commitment. Start by imagining a pantry, like you might have in your kitchen (or remember from TV shows about life on the prairie). Imagine the shelves empty for the moment. Now, think about some value you hold. Give yourself a few minutes to roll the value around in your head while you consider the following question: If you were going to stock your pantry with acts, both big and small, that would serve this value, what would they be? Put each of these acts into a mason jar or brown paper and place them one by one onto the shelves.

Do you value being a great partner? Maybe your first jar contains a greeting at the front door after your love comes home from a hard day. The second might be a promise to listen calmly next time the two of you have a quarrel. On another shelf, maybe there's a little box that contains a time when you will cheerfully agree to the movie or the restaurant of your partner's choice. Just let your pantry fill up with acts you can do. If you fill up one pantry, consider another value and stock up on it as well.

Seen from an ACT perspective, then, there's much more to commitment than just making promises about what will happen tomorrow or the next day. In contrast to the everyday, fixed-and-future sense of commitment, committed action from an ACT perspective involves an ongoing, in-the-moment process of choosing and rechoosing the directions in which we'll move. This nuanced commitment is a dynamic process rather than a static fact, and it has the potential to show up for us in each unfolding moment. More than being a measuring stick for our successes and failures, this kind of commitment is a skill we can refine that will help us reach our goal of finding the freedom to live a rich and meaningful life.

Commitment—Right Now

Commitment is another area where there's an affinity and intimacy between process areas. If commitment seems to resonate with what we said about present-moment contact, you're getting a good feel for this stuff. The breathing meditation game we described a while back is a very apt metaphor for the kind of commitment we're talking about. If you consider your experiences following your breath, you can observe what commitment from this perspective looks like in flight.

When you sit down to do breathing meditation, you choose your breath as something to pay attention to. You get comfortable, and you start to breathe. One, two, three—and then you feel a pain in your hip, and off goes your attention. So you find it and gently bring it back to your breath. One, two, three—and now here comes the thought about whether you remembered to pay the electric bill. Once again, you recognize your inattention. You meet it with kindness, like a familiar friend you meet in the street. You say hello, linger for a moment, and then go back on your way, returning to your breath. You do this because concentration on your breath is what you *chose* to do. In this gentle yet persistent return to your chosen direction, you'll find the very heart of what we mean when we talk about commitment from an ACT perspective.

Committing to Values, Valuing Commitment

Keep the details of the last chapter close as you consider this idea of commitment. From an ACT perspective, committed action isn't terribly different from your values. In fact, many aspects of life where you might identify values—things such as being a parent, excelling at a profession, or being a good friend—are likely to involve making and keeping commitments. When this is the case, commitment can be viewed as part of valuing.

Take a value that may very well be important to you: being a good parent. There are certain patterns of behavior you might associate with being a good parent. You might point to providing for your children, spending time with them, encouraging them to explore the world, and so forth. If you thought about it for a while, you could probably put together a pretty specific and detailed list of what being a good parent looks like for you.

If you think back over your life for the past couple of weeks, can you say you always acted in a manner consistent with the value you hold about being a good parent? If you didn't, welcome. You're in good company with all of the rest of us who set our sights on something, fall short of the mark, dust ourselves off, and reach out for it one more time. Sometimes we'll be perfectly in line with what we value. Other days, other moments, we'll find ourselves at odds with our values. In that moment, the moment in which we notice that we're out of alignment with one of our values, can we pause, notice our dislocation, and gently return? It's difficult to imagine a value of any magnitude that will not involve a lifetime of gentle returns. This turning back makes all the difference.

8

You

Are

Large,

You

Contain

Multitudes:

Self-as-Context

The past and present wilt—I have fill'd them, emptied them.

And proceed to fill my next fold of the future.

Listener up there! What have you to confide to me?

Look in my face while I snuff the sidle of evening.

(Talk honestly; no one else hears you, and I stay only a minute.)

Do I contradict myself?

Very well then, I contradict myself.

(I am large; I contain multitudes.)

—Walt Whitman, *Leaves of Grass*

We wrap up our discussion with a process area that revolves around the answer to the question, "Who are you?" We ask this question in a very restricted way. We're not talking about everyday questions of identity, the kind you could resolve by looking at your driver's license or asking your mother. And we're also not talking about very esoteric questions of identity that require the languages of spirituality or speculative science to answer. For our purposes, it's all the same whether your physical body is comprised mostly of empty space traversed by electrons in uncertain locations or of cosmic light.

What we're interested in is your conception of self from a psychological perspective—and really, we're not even interested in that in a broad sense. For the purposes of our discussion, we're going to call effective functioning in this process area *self-as-context*. From this positive, functional perspective, the answer to the question "Who are you?" would be something like, "I'm the person who has experienced all of the thoughts, feelings, bodily states, and external events that make up my life. I'm also the context in which all of the future events of my life will unfold." The corresponding, problematic function of this process area is *self-as-content*. From this less flexible perspective, the answer to the question "Who are you?" would, instead, be something to the effect of, "I'm a bad son, the kind of person who doesn't call home often enough," "I'm a crazy person," or "I'm the guy who's always on the bottom, so I need to fight to get to the top." More broadly—and more abstractly—self-as-context is identification with the ongoing process of being conscious, and self-as-content is identification with the contents of consciousness.

Sound familiar? It should. Self-as-context, as a perspective, is characterized by the dynamic qualities of inclusivity, fluidity, and evolution. In its inclusivity it's reminiscent of acceptance, of making the conscious choice to engage with all aspects of your experience rather than clinging to some and excluding others. In its fluidity, self-as-context recalls defusion, when you engage with your thoughts the way water engages with a stone in its path, by washing over and around it rather than grabbing it and holding on for dear life. And our discussion of values really hinged on their evolving quality, their capacity to change with you all throughout your life.

If you reverse all of these descriptions, you'll get a reasonable definition for self-as-content—and for avoidance, fusion, and absent or fixed values as well. Here you would have an experience of life dominated by a strong urge to push away and exclude painful experiences, to cling to your thoughts as if they were absolutely true and immutable, and to stay exactly the same for ever and ever. From a self-as-content perspective, it's very easy to regard your experiences with anxiety—especially if they've been particularly painful and disruptive—almost like a death sentence. And, honestly, this kind of closed-up and limiting perspective is very common to people with problems in living—and this means *all* people, whether anxiety is a part of their lives or not. But if a self-as-content perspective can feel like a death sentence, the good news is that a self-as-context perspective can rather quickly start to feel like a reprieve.

"Self" as a Verb

As we suggested just a little bit ago, there are certainly other ways to understand self and identity than the one we're proposing. The narrow sense we're using here really points toward the role your sense of who you are plays in your interactions with the world and the choices you make. From an ACT perspective, identity or a sense of self is not connected to a fixed idea that exists somehow removed from experience. Rather, it's the summation of a stream of acts, choices, and perceptions. It's really more accurate to think of your sense of self as your "act of self-ing" from this perspective. The creation of your identity is an ongoing, dynamic process that continues to take place for as long as you keep breathing.

The process of defining this sense of self starts for all of us very early in life—before we can even hold our heads up on our own. Over time, we're asked many, many questions about how we perceive the world and how others perceive it. What did you have for breakfast? What did your brother have? Your sister wants ice cream. What do you want? Where were you this morning? What's your favorite color? Through this series of questions, we learn to answer from a relatively consistent perspective.

Like any behavioral pattern, however, it's not entirely fixed. Our position in space, time, and circumstance changes what we see, feel, and think—and, importantly, our sense of who we are. When you were seven, maybe you thought that getting to pick your own flavor of breakfast cereal was the *absolute end*! But now, with your own income and access to every cereal on the market, it probably doesn't matter to you so much whether you have to buy generic cornflakes or a national brand.

Sometimes, though, we all fall into repetitive patterns of responding that, over time, make us progressively less sensitive to context. Anxiety can be part of such a repetitive pattern. If unease and fear overwhelm you in social situations—from one gathering to another, for years and years—you'll be likely to dump all social situations into a big mental file folder and label it "bad," regardless of the fact that many of them will be dissimilar. One is a dinner party of old friends, and another a conference of your professional colleagues. Still another is a gang of other parents from your kid's school who sometimes get together for coffee. When you see it written out, you can probably imagine contextual differences among these three, but a long pattern of relatively rigid responding to "social situations" can make you treat them as one and the same. You become "the sort of person who doesn't do well in social situations." In other words, your sense of who you are and who you might become gets locked down in content.

Letting Go of You as an Anxious Person

The self-as-context process makes contact with your experience of anxiety most significantly when you consider the question, "Am I an anxious person?" The way you answer this question and the way you organize your activities around that answer can have a huge impact on your experience of life. This is especially true if you've had a long history of struggle with anxiety.

If your sense of self is the product of an ongoing stream of events and choices that could be expressed as conclusions to the statement, "I...," the toll on that sense of a lifetime's worth of anxiety is likely to be profound:

- I need to keep my toys off the floor. What if Daddy yells at me again?

- I don't know all of the state capitals. What if I get called on and look like a fool?

- I'll skip the prom. If I ask her to the dance and she laughs at me, I'll just die.

- I'll forget about applying for that job. If I had to interview, I wouldn't know what to say.

- I'll keep the kids home from school. What if they catch the flu from one of the other children?

140

You can almost feel the edges of this life closing in with each new experience. Remember that humans like to make up categories and then put things into them. Experiences like the ones above point toward the category "anxious person." And what do anxious people do? They stay out of elevators, avoid going to the doctor, refrain from public speaking, skip parties...

Do you see how this works? How life quickly gets bound up with content about who we are and what we can become? If you've come to think of yourself as an anxious person, a change in perspective about who you are and what you can become would be a major step toward liberating you from anxiety.

Walking a Mile in (Your Own) Shoes

Sounds good, right? So how do you do it? In a way, this entire book has been a long lesson in how to adopt a self-as-context perspective. If you can learn to remain connected to what's going on in your life right now, accepting both the sweet and the sad, holding lightly the stories about what's possible while turning your actions toward things that matter to you, you'll have pretty much solved the riddle of self-as-context. We said early on in the book that all of the processes are reflected in each other, and this is what it pretty much comes down to: anything and everything you do that expands your possibilities in any of the six process areas discussed in this book will very likely open up more space in all of them. While this doesn't for a moment imply that it's easy or effortless to make these changes—old habits, after all, die hard—the path this thinking points to is at least pretty clear.

If we want to get specific about self-as-context, though, the way to do it is through some active perspective taking. In other words, we imagine what the world might look like if we could look at it from a different vantage point. The change in perspective can involve shifting time, space, or even identity. Whatever form it takes, the act of trying to see the world through a different pair of eyes gives you a chance to practice feeling what it's like to be open to different sets of possibilities.

If you've spent a lifetime locked down with feelings of anxiety about, let's say, getting on an airplane, it might be all but impossible for you to imagine hopping on the 11:30 flight bound for Kansas City. You might be "the kind of person who never flies," and your racing heart and sweaty palms at the thought of being "someone who might fly in a particular context" might provide enough disincentive for you to avoid even considering the idea.

But what if you weren't *you*? What if you were that guy down the street who's a flight attendant? What would your life look like then? Or maybe you're you, but you're the you who, at the age of eight, couldn't wait to fly to see Grandma in Florida and, after you got home, refused to take the plastic pilot's wings off your shirt for a month? Or what if you were you just as you are, but you found yourself talking to a scared child? What if she needed to fly to Memphis for treatment at St. Jude's hospital, but she was terrified to be so high up in the air? What would you say to her?

Trying on some different perspectives can open you up to new ways of being in the world. If you're struggling with anxiety, this kind of practice can help you start to imagine a world where you can live your life the way you choose, even with feelings of anxiety— regardless of whether the possibility seems impossible to you at the moment. Here's a little game you can play that might get you started with perspective taking.

Game: Letter from the Future
Props: Pen and paper or your computer •
Difficulty: Somewhat hard

This game is played in two rounds. You'll complete each round by writing a short letter—just the kind of friendly correspondence you might put on a postcard or in an e-mail. Your objective in each round is to explore the world from a slightly different perspective than the one you currently have, although the nature of that difference varies from the first round to the second.

Preparation: If you like to write with a pen and paper, set yourself up at a table or desk with these tools at hand. If you're a committed typist, you can sit down in front of your computer (or your IBM Selectric, if you think this whole personal computer thing is just a fad). Before you write or type anything, though, close your eyes and take a few deep breaths, settling yourself in your chair. Without trying very hard to think of anything in particular, allow something that you've been bothered about for a long time to come into your thoughts. Since you've been at this book for quite a while, this will likely be some problem with anxiety. Maybe it's a tendency to worry all the time about things like financial security or your health. Perhaps it's a specific fear that causes you lots of problems. Whatever it is, call it to mind and sit with it for a few moments.

Round 1: With your eyes closed, take a few moments to imagine a child. If you're male, imagine a boy, and if you're female, imagine a girl. In either case, picture a child of about ten years of age. Let yourself see this child clearly. Now imagine that this child comes to you and tells you that he or she is troubled about the same problem you're concerned about. If your troubling thought isn't age appropriate for a child—for example, if you're worried about your finances or job security—you can imagine that the child is responding to things his or her parents have mentioned along these lines. Let yourself see the pain and concern in the child's face, hear it in his or her voice. Allow yourself to connect as deeply as possible with this other human being who is in pain. This child's pain is similar to your own, but at such a young age, he or she is likely less able to make sense of it, and more vulnerable to its consequences. Breathe deeply as you consider the whole situation.

Now imagine that your time with this child is very short. In fact, all you can give the child is a letter that he or she can take along on a long journey. Do you want this letter to be a source of comfort? Of support? If you only had the space on the back of a postcard or a few sheets of notebook paper, what would you tell this child who's hurting?

Think about this for as long as you like, and then write your letter.

Round 2: Start this round of the game by imagining yourself in ten years. No one knows what will happen in the future, but you can imagine it any way you want. The goal here is *not* necessarily to imagine a rosy world in which you've conquered your every trouble. Rather, you should try to imagine a wiser, more seasoned you. Try to imagine in some detail your life as it will be in a decade: Where will you live? What will you be doing? What will your daily experiences look like?

Once you've imagined those details for a little while, try to look back at yourself in the present from the perspective of you in the future. How does your life now appear to the you from ten years hence? Do you feel sympathy for yourself? Concern and compassion?

Explore this situation for a little while with your eyes closed. Then, when you're ready, write another letter. This time, you'll write the letter from the perspective of your future self, and you'll address yourself in the present. What will you tell yourself? Again, will you offer words of kindness, compassion, and support? Will you offer advice to persevere, to not give up hope?

When you're finished with both rounds, save both of your letters. Set them aside for a while—a few days or weeks. At some point, take a look at what you wrote. Consider for a time what it meant to you to think about your situation in life from a different perspective? Wonder how you might live your life differently right now if you could let yourself look at things through a slightly different lens.

New Beginnings

This whole business of seeing yourself as a stage on which your life unfolds, rather than as a set of rules and restrictions according to which your life must proceed, might be something completely new for you. If it is, we think it's likely that it'll make a big difference in the way you take in and interact with the world around you. We also think it might make a significant difference in the way you approach your life in light of your experience with anxiety. That anxious thoughts have had a limiting effect on your life for a long time is a fact, fixed in time and unchangeable. Whether they continue to box you in and block you from the things in your life that matter is still very much an open question. If you're the context in which your life unfolds, each new moment is an opportunity to set out on a course bound for richness, meaning, and purpose. Anxiety might lie along the way, but it doesn't need to be an insurmountable hurdle in getting you where you want to go.

9

Things
Still
Might Go
Terribly,
Horribly
Wrong

We don't like long good-byes. And we've pretty much said all we wanted to say. No need for any grand finale here.

Not to mention, last chapters of books, like the last lines of poems, are really more like birthdays than burials. The end of your first reading marks the beginning of your life with the story in your head and, if it was good, in your heart. From here, it's your job to take what you found, sift through it, and decide what you want to use to change your life.

Back in the very first chapter, we made a big deal out of the fact that ACT can't protect you from the world—and to the extent that the world includes planes crashing into buildings on Tuesday mornings and tsunamis washing away the breakfast table on Boxing Day, this is true. This place and time we share is cut through with loves that fade, pink slips, moldy strawberries, dark shapes on X-rays, fleas, stray bullets, Ponzi schemes, revenge plots gone wrong, and death camps. Horrors, both big and small, abound. If you feel anxious, if you sit around on tenterhooks waiting for things to go terribly, horribly wrong—well, it's not as if you have no reason, is it?

Standing side by side with all this horror, though, is abundance, joy, and love in inconceivable measure. Sometimes people do grow old in each other's arms, heroes really do save the day, and the dog does come home on its own after being gone for three days. Children laugh in the streets, and birds sing. Crisp white sheets smell just a little of bleach, and the first mouthful of coffee in the morning tastes like blueberries and chocolate. Just once, when you've bothered to bring an umbrella, it actually does rain.

What if there *was* something that could protect you from the world? Imagine that we could write you a book that offered some talking points and exercises that, once completed, would cure you of your anxiety—but with a catch. Your worry, panic, and fear would be gone, but any excitement, contentment, and joy you might feel would go along with it. Your experience of life would be safe and colorless and flat. We could protect you from the bad but only at the expense of the good.

Would you buy that book? If you've been in pain long enough and severely enough, you might. A lot of people opt for something similar, although that cure is usually delivered by the glass or the dose rather than in pages and paragraphs. Numbness is certainly an option, although the cost that comes with it is pretty steep.

Implicit in this whole book has been the assumption that embracing life—all of life—is ultimately more rewarding than trying to weed out those experiences that we would rather avoid. The work we do in ACT is about finding a way to open up, to take it all in, to find the flexibility we need to work around obstacles in the world and inside our own heads that stand between us and what we want. Giving you a taste of this has been our mission in the pages you've just read. We hope you enjoyed reading it, and we hope it helps.

But wait! We didn't tell you what to *do* when you feel anxious! What kind of self-help book is this without a toolbox of sure-fire techniques you can use in the moment to do this and that...

Well, honestly, we're not really all that good at giving tips and bulleted lists. But if what we've written here has touched you at all, here's our one in-the-moment exercise you can try when you find yourself feeling anxious. It might prove useful to you.

1. Whatever you're doing, slow down. Silly slow. Comically slow. Slur your words; pretend you're a sloth. Whatever it takes, go really, really slow.

2. On the inside of the front cover of this book, there's a question. It reads: In this very moment, will you accept the sad and the sweet, hold lightly stories about what's possible, and be the author of a life that has meaning and purpose for you, turning in kindness back to that life when you find yourself moving away from it?

3. Don't try to answer the question right away. Instead, just linger inside it without answering. Read the question aloud, word by word, listening carefully and taking a moment to let each word and phrase sink in.

4. Then, in some small way, answer the question with your life. Make one small act that would be a kindness in your life. Make one small offering to a value that is your own.

And with that, we'll leave you with a parting thought, a poem that touched us. We hope it touches you, too.

At times we feel the need to go back
to plain things. To stones, earth,

grass, wind. To things we have known
a long time, to what we knew

when what filled the hours was dirt
and a few sticks, a pile of leaves

or some thin, white bones
from a long-dead bird.

The huge rock near the creek
was not too hard to lie on then

and the sun on bare skin felt warm.
We did not feel the press of time

as we do now. The world seemed firm
and real, and life was slow, and long, and good.

—Carolyn Elkins, "What We Knew"

Sources

for

Further

Study

Each of us has a little different idea about how much is enough to know about something. Some of us like to dive deeply into ideas; others prefer to take a set of guidelines and learn how they work by putting them through their paces. We're tempted to think that, because you decided to read a book about anxiety rather than, say, skim the Wikipedia article on the subject, you're probably more closely allied with the former camp.

Acceptance and Commitment Therapy

Five years ago your choices for reading about ACT were pretty limited. Not so today. The body of literature on ACT, both for professionals and general readers, has grown steadily over the last few years. If you're interested in this approach, you have a great variety of books on the subject from which to choose. Each of the following books and its authors come at the basic concepts in ACT differently, so reading widely from this list will give you a good flavor for the whole scope of the work.

Steven C. Hayes's workbook with Spencer Smith, *Get Out of Your Mind and Into Your Life: The New Acceptance and Commitment Therapy* (New Harbinger, 2005), is a good all-around introduction to ACT that doesn't necessarily focus on any one kind of mental health problem. *The Mindfulness and Acceptance Workbook for Anxiety: A Guide to Breaking Free from Anxiety, Phobias, and Worry Using Acceptance and Commitment Therapy* (New Harbinger, 2008), by John P. Forsyth and Georg H. Eifert, comes at the problem of anxiety from a slightly different angle than *Things Might Go Terribly, Horribly Wrong*, but like this book, it's aimed at problems with anxiety. In addition to a number of pen-and-paper exercises, *The Mindfulness and Acceptance Workbook* comes with an audio CD with some useful and interesting guided meditations. Finally, among the books written for general readers, Chad LeJeune's *The Worry Trap: How to Free Yourself from Worry and Anxiety Using Acceptance and Commitment Therapy*

(New Harbinger, 2007) is focused specifically on the condition of persistent worry known as generalized anxiety disorder.

Much of what you've just read in this book was anticipated in our book *Mindfulness for Two* (New Harbinger, 2008), but in that volume, we go into greater detail about the behavior science that grounds this stuff. *Mindfulness for Two* is pretty readable for a professional book. If you think you want to explore the foundations of ACT a little further, we think you might want to take a look.

If you *really* take an interest in ACT and want to learn more about the theory and basic behavioral science that make it tick, you might want to take a look at the 1999 book from The Guilford Press titled *Acceptance and Commitment Therapy: An Experiential Approach to Behavior Change.* Kelly was one of the authors, along with Steven C. Hayes and Kirk D. Strosahl, on this groundbreaking volume, which was the first book to document the structure and practice of ACT. As we write this, the 1999 book is in the process of revision, and a new edition of the book is expected from Guilford sometime in 2010. Like any book written for academics, *Acceptance and Commitment Therapy* requires, well, a commitment to get through—but it can be a worthwhile read if this work really speaks to you.

Finally, you might want to pay a visit to the website of the professional organization that connects the world ACT community, the Association for Contextual Behavior Science, or ACBS. Unlike a lot of professional organization sites, ACBS's website has a lot of information that might be of interest to folks who aren't professionals. A good place to land is on the "ACT for the Public" page at www. contextualpsychology.org/act_for_the_public. ACBS also maintains a directory of ACT therapists on their site, should you find yourself thinking about taking your relationship with this work to the next level.

If what you've read in *Things* has been of use to you, we encourage you to visit the ACT for the Public pages and other public forums and talk about your experiences.

Mindfulness

The concept of mindfulness is an ancient one. In two thousand years, there's a lot of time for writing books. Unsurprisingly, there are literally dozens of wonderful books to choose from if you want to learn more about opening up to the present moment. Jon Kabat-Zinn is a singular figure in the contemporary study of mindfulness, and his work has had a profound and personal influence on both of us. His books *Coming to Our Senses: Healing Ourselves and the World Through Mindfulness* (Hyperion, 2006) and *Wherever You Go, There You Are: Mindfulness Meditation in Everyday Life* (Hyperion, 2005) are both wonderful, and they only scratch the surface of the works available from this gifted teacher. While there's almost no end to the Buddhist books on the subject of mindfulness, *The Miracle of Mindfulness* (Beacon Press, 1999) and *The Heart of the Buddha's Teaching: Transforming Suffering into Peace, Joy, and Liberation* (Broadway, 1999), by Thich Nhat Hanh, are accessible books that offer a good introduction to the subject.

Calming Your Anxious Mind: How Mindfulness and Compassion Can Free You from Anxiety, Fear, and Panic (New Harbinger, 2007), by Jeffrey Brantley, a psychiatrist at the Duke University Center for Integrative Medicine, is a clear and useful application of mindfulness to the task of moving past anxiety. It's well worth a read if you find yourself interested in how building this kind of practice might help you live well with feelings of anxiety.

Other Wonderful Books

You might have noticed that we have a thing for poetry. One thing we've noticed over time is that, inside the work of poets we love are lessons about living we can find if we're willing to sit with the poem long enough and quietly enough to find them. In this book, you'll find the work of T. S. Eliot, Robert Burns, Matthew Arnold, William Butler Yeats, Emily Dickinson, Elizabeth Bishop, Walt Whitman, Alfred Lord Tennyson, Carolyn Elkins, the authors of the King James Bible, and Shakespeare. We also have some lines from Lenny Bruce and Samuel Beckett on the prose side of things. Instead of recommending volumes for these poets and writers, we'll refer you to our reference section if you want to know which editions we were reading. If you just want to read any of these folks, you have only to drop by your local library or browse the works that are all over the Internet.

References

Abbott, B. B. 1985. Rats prefer signaled over unsignaled shock-free periods. *Journal of Experimental Psychology: Animal Behavior Processes* 11 (2):215–23.

American Psychiatric Association. 2000. *Diagnostic and Statistical Manual of Mental Disorders (DSM-IV-TR)*. 4th ed. (text rev.) Washington, DC: American Psychiatric Association.

Arnold, M. 1998. *Matthew Arnold: Selected Poems*. New York: Everyman.

Badia, P., J. Harsh, and B. Abbott. 1979. Choosing between predictable and unpredictable shock conditions: Data and theory. *Psychological Bulletin* 86 (5):1107–31.

Beckett, S. 1996. *Nohow On: Company, Ill Seen Ill said, Worstward Ho—Three Novels*. New York: Grove Press.

Bishop, E. 1984. *Elizabeth Bishop: The Complete Poems, 1927–1979*. New York: Farrar, Straus, and Giroux.

Bruce, L. 1992. *How to Talk Dirty and Influence People: An Autobiography*. New York: Fireside.

Burns, R. 1991. *Poems and Songs*. New York: Dover Thrift.

Calleo, J., and M. Stanley. 2008. Anxiety disorders in later life: Differentiated diagnosis and treatment strategies. *Psychiatric Times* 25 (8). www.psychiatrictimes.com/anxiety/article/10168/1166976. Accessed 14 July 2009.

Centers for Disease Control and Prevention, National Center for Inquiry Prevention and Control. n.d. Web-based injury statistics query and reporting system (WISQARS). www.cdc.gov/injury/wisqars/index.html (accessed May 14, 2009).

Chase, D. 2002. *The Sopranos: Selected Scripts from Three Seasons*. New York: Home Box Office.

Chiles, J. A., and K. D. Strosahl. 2005. *Clinical Manual for Assessment and Treatment of Suicidal Patients*. Arlington, VA: American Psychiatric Publishing, Inc.

Dickinson, E. 1976. *The Complete Poems of Emily Dickinson.* Ed. T. H. Johnson. New York: Back Bay Books.

Elkins, C. 2002. *Daedalus Rising.* Greenville, SC: Emrys Press.

Eliot, T. S. 1991. *Collected Poems, 1909–1962.* Orlando, FL: Harcourt Brace and Company.

Frankl, V. E. 1959. *Man's Search for Meaning: An Introduction to Logotherapy.* Boston, MA: Beacon Press.

Kabat-Zinn, J. 1994. *Wherever You Go, There You Are: Mindfulness Meditation in Everyday Life.* New York: Hyperion.

Kessler, R. C., W. T. Chiu, O. Demler, and E. E. Walters. 2005. Prevalence, severity, and comorbidity of twelve-month DSM-IV disorders in the National Comorbidity Survey Replication (NCS-R). *Archives of General Psychiatry* 62 (6):617–27.

Kessler, R. C., K. A. McGonagle, S. Zhao, C. B. Nelson, M. Hughes, S. Eshleman, H. U. Wittchen, and K. S. Kendler. 1994. Lifetime and 12-month prevalence of *DSM-III-R* psychiatric disorders in the United States. Results from the National Comorbidity Survey. *Archives of General Psychiatry* 51 (1):8–19.

Moore, S. 1985. *Let This Mind Be in You: The Quest for Identity Through Oedipus to Christ.* Minneapolis, MN: Winston Press.

Schmich, M. 1997. Advice, like youth, probably just wasted on the young. *Chicago Tribune,* June 1.

Shakespeare, W. 1996. *The Riverside Shakespeare.* 2nd ed. Ed. G. B. Evans and J. J. M. Tobin. New York: Houghton Mifflin Company.

Sinatra, F. 2008. *Sinatra: Nothing but the Best.* Los Angeles: Reprise Records.

Tennyson, A. L. 1985. *Tennyson: Selected Poetry.* New York: Penguin Books.

Whitman, W. 1998. *The Complete Poems of Walt Whitman*. London: Wordsworth Editions.

Wood, J. V., W. Q. Perunovic, and J. W. Lee. 2009. Positive self-statements: Power for some, peril for others. *Psychological Science* 20 (7):860–66.

Yeats, W. B. 1996. *The Collected Poems of W. B. Yeats*. 2nd rev. ed. Ed. R. J. Finneran. New York: Scribner.

KELLY G. WILSON, PhD, is associate professor of psychology at the University of Mississippi. He is coauthor of the seminal book *Acceptance and Commitment Therapy*, which set the foundation for this new model of psychotherapy, as well at the book *Mindfulness for Two*. He lives and works in Oxford, MS.

www.onelifellc.com

TROY DUFRENE is a writer specializing in psychology. He is coauthor of *Coping with OCD* and *Mindfulness for Two*. He lives and works in Oakland, CA.

www.troydufrene.com

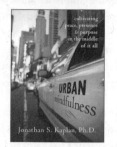
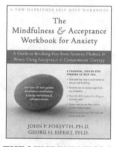
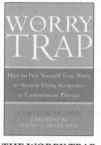

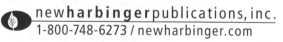

FROM OUR PUBLISHER—

As the publisher at New Harbinger and a clinical psychologist since 1978, I know that emotional problems are best helped with evidence-based therapies. These are the treatments derived from scientific research (randomized controlled trials) that show what works. Whether these treatments are delivered by trained clinicians or found in a self-help book, they are designed to provide you with proven strategies to overcome your problem.

Therapies that aren't evidence-based—whether offered by clinicians or in books—are much less likely to help. In fact, therapies that aren't guided by science may not help you at all. That's why this New Harbinger book is based on scientific evidence that the treatment can relieve emotional pain.

This is important: if this book isn't enough, and you need the help of a skilled therapist, use the following resources to find a clinician trained in the evidence-based protocols appropriate for your problem. And if you need more support— a community that understands what you're going through and can show you ways to cope—resources for that are provided below, as well.

Real help is available for the problems you have been struggling with. The skills you can learn from evidence-based therapies will change your life.

new harbinger
CELEBRATING
40 YEARS

Matthew McKay, PhD
Publisher, New Harbinger Publications

If you need a therapist, the following organization can help you find a therapist trained in acceptance and commitment therapy (ACT).

Association for Contextual Behavioral Science (ACBS)
please visit www.contextualscience.org and click on *Find an ACT Therapist*.

For additional support for patients, family, and friends, please contact the following:

Anxiety and Depression Association of American (ADAA)
please visit www.adaa.org

National Alliance on Mental Illness (NAMI)
please visit www.nami.org
